KATELYN OHASHI

From Olympic Hopeful to Body Positivity Advocate: The Untold Story of Her Rise Beyond Gymnastics

Robert N. Marsh

Copyright © 2024 by Robert N. Marsh

All rights reserved. No part of this publication may be reproduced, distributed, or transmitted in any form or by any means, including photocopying, recording, or other electronic or mechanical methods, without the prior written permission of the publisher, except in the case of brief quotations embodied in critical reviews and certain other noncommercial uses permitted by copyright law.

DISCLAIMER

This book is a biographical account of Katelyn Ohashi, based on thorough research, interviews, public records, and material available at the time of publication. Every effort has been made to ensure the accuracy of the information, though some details may be open to interpretation. Names, trademarks, and registered trademarks belong to their respective owners and are referenced only for clarity, with no intent to infringe upon their rights. This book is not officially endorsed by or associated with any organizations or governing bodies mentioned. The author and publisher are not responsible for any errors or omissions and will not be held legally accountable for any damages, losses, or financial implications resulting from the information provided, either directly or indirectly.

TABLE OF CONTENTS

INTRODUCTION 1

Chapter 1: The Early Years 4
   Katelyn's Childhood in Seattle 4
   Early Training and the Support of Her Family 7
   The Path to Junior Elite Gymnastics 11

Chapter 2: Rising Through the Ranks 16
   Competing at the Highest Level 16
   National Titles and International Recognition 19
   The Burden of Expectations 22

Chapter 3: Injuries and Setbacks 27
   A Promising Career Halted by Injury 27
   Dealing with Pain, Recovery, and the Reality of Missing the Olympics 30
   Reflecting on the Mental and Physical Toll of Elite Gymnastics 34

Chapter 4: A New Beginning 38
   Transitioning to Collegiate Gymnastics 38
   Coach Valorie Kondos Field's Influence 41
   Balancing School, Training, and Life Beyond Gymnastics 45

Chapter 5: The Perfect 10 50
   Crafting the Iconic Floor Routine 50
   The Moment of Perfection 53
   The Media Frenzy and Global Recognition 56

Chapter 6: Battling Body Image and Mental Health Challenges 61
   Behind the Scenes 61
   Breaking the Silence 64
   Embracing Body Positivity 68

Chapter 7: Becoming an Advocate 72
  Speaking Out on Mental Health 72
  Advocating for Body Positivity 75
  Inspiring the Next Generation 79

Chapter 8: Life Beyond the Mat 83
  Retirement from Gymnastics 83
  Exploring New Avenues 86
  Adjusting to Life Without Elite Competition 90

Chapter 9: Impact on Gymnastics and Pop Culture 94
  How Katelyn's Story Has Changed Gymnastics Culture 94
  The Shift in Media Representation of Female Athletes 97
  Her Lasting Legacy 101

Chapter 10: The Ongoing Journey 105
  Continuing Her Advocacy for Mental Health and Body Image 105
  Lessons Learned from Her Journey 108
  Katelyn's Vision for the Future and Her Role as a Changemaker 112

CONCLUSION 116

INTRODUCTION

Katelyn Ohashi's journey from Olympic hopeful to global advocate for body positivity is remarkable and transformative. Known initially for her incredible talent as a gymnast, Katelyn's rise to fame involved much more than her performances on the mat. Her story extends beyond gymnastics, exploring themes of personal growth, resilience, and the powerful message of self-acceptance. Katelyn's career, marked by triumphs and challenges, illustrates how an individual can break free from expectations to lead a movement grounded in authenticity and empowerment.

In the world of elite gymnastics, athletes are often placed under enormous pressure to meet stringent physical and aesthetic standards. Katelyn's rise in the sport came with immense expectations, as she was once on the path to becoming an Olympic star. Her talent and dedication were evident from a young age, propelling her into the spotlight as a promising gymnast with a desirable future. However, the demands of maintaining perfection in performance and appearance would soon weigh heavily on her, revealing a side of gymnastics often hidden from public view.

It was during this time that Katelyn began to grapple with her self-image and mental health as the toll of the sport's high expectations started to affect her well-being. Her decision to step away from elite competition surprised many but also began a personal transformation that would redefine her legacy. Katelyn prioritized her mental and emotional health, a bold step that would inspire countless others to do the same. In sharing her story, she became a voice for those facing similar pressures, advocating for a more supportive environment within sports and beyond.

Katelyn's return to gymnastics through collegiate competition marked a new chapter, where she performed with a renewed sense of joy and freedom. Her viral floor routine, which captured the world's attention in 2019, became an emblem of her personal and professional evolution. Without chasing perfection, Katelyn embraced her individuality and love for the sport, showcasing a performance that radiated skill and happiness. It was a moment that transcended the sport, symbolizing a shift in how athletes are viewed, not just for their achievements but for their humanity.

This book, "Katelyn Ohashi: From Olympic Hopeful to Body Positivity Advocate," delves deep into the untold aspects of her journey, focusing not just on the gymnastics world but on her broader impact. Katelyn's advocacy for body positivity and mental health has extended far beyond the athletic community, resonating with people of all ages and backgrounds. Her story offers a candid exploration of athletes' pressures and how breaking free from those expectations can lead to a more meaningful and fulfilling path.

Through her advocacy work, public speaking, and personal stories, Katelyn has shed light on the unrealistic standards imposed on athletes, especially women, and the detrimental effects these pressures can have on self-esteem and mental well-being. She has become a prominent figure in conversations about body image, encouraging others to embrace their true selves regardless of societal norms or expectations. Her message challenges the traditional narrative of success, particularly within sports, and promotes the idea that true achievement lies in personal happiness and self-acceptance.

This book will explore Katelyn's early years in gymnastics, the pivotal moments that led her to question the demands placed upon her and the turning points that allowed her to rise beyond the confines of her sport. It will also highlight her role as a changemaker in the broader cultural conversation surrounding body image and mental health, illustrating how her influence has inspired a new generation of athletes and individuals.

Katelyn Ohashi's story is more than just one of athletic prowess; it is a testament to the power of self-discovery and the courage to stand against deeply ingrained ideals. As we explore her life and the lessons she has shared with the world, this book aims to provide a deeper understanding of the person behind the viral moments and the athlete who chose authenticity over conformity. Through her ongoing work, Katelyn inspires a movement toward greater acceptance and compassion, both on and off the mat.

As we will uncover, her legacy is not just about gymnastics or medals; it's about the way she has used her platform to advocate for a healthier, more inclusive definition of success. This is the untold story of how Katelyn Ohashi rose beyond gymnastics, becoming a voice for body positivity, mental health, and authenticity.

Chapter 1: The Early Years

Katelyn's Childhood in Seattle

Katelyn Ohashi's journey began in Seattle, Washington, where her vibrant personality and boundless energy found an outlet in the world of gymnastics. Born into a supportive family, Katelyn was the youngest of four children. Her mother, a former high school gymnast, was pivotal in introducing her to the sport at a young age. When Katelyn first stepped into a gym, it became apparent that she had an unusual enthusiasm for movement. Before formally starting gymnastics, her natural agility and keen interest in flipping, tumbling, and bouncing around her home indicated a love for physical activity that needed a structured outlet.

An intense curiosity about the world around her marked her early years. Katelyn was an active and fearless child, never hesitant to try new things or push her physical limits. This fearless spirit translated seamlessly into her gymnastics training when she began formal lessons. Encouraged by her mother, Katelyn entered a local gym where her energetic nature found focus. Her first exposure to organized training was filled with excitement and joy, emotions that would become trademarks of her career. She was captivated by the freedom that gymnastics provided, the sense that she could twist and turn in ways that felt both liberating and exhilarating.

From the beginning, her coaches noticed something special in her. While most children explore a sport with tentative steps, Katelyn approached it with a confidence that belied her age. She was unafraid to try difficult skills, and though her technique was far from polished at the start, her enthusiasm set her apart. Katelyn's early coaches described her as a bundle of energy eager to learn and improve. This relentless drive would become a key part of her identity as an athlete, fueling her rise in the sport.

Beyond the gym, Katelyn's family played a crucial role in shaping her early experiences with gymnastics. Her mother, who understood the intricacies of the sport from her own experiences, became Katelyn's first supporter and mentor. Her siblings also shared her journey, often attending her practices and competitions. This environment of encouragement provided Katelyn with the stability and support she needed to flourish. While her family encouraged her passion, they also instilled in her the importance of balance, ensuring that she did not lose sight of the joy that initially drew her to the sport.

As Katelyn's love for gymnastics deepened, her commitment to the sport grew. By age six, she was training several hours a week, a schedule that required significant dedication for someone so young. Yet, Katelyn was never deterred. Her coaches continued to notice her remarkable work ethic and positive attitude. She showed an unusual ability to maintain focus during long training sessions, balancing her natural exuberance with impressive discipline. At an age when many children were still developing their basic motor skills, Katelyn was mastering more complex maneuvers, leaving an impression on everyone around her.

Her rapid progress did not go unnoticed in the larger gymnastics community. By age eight, Katelyn had already begun competing in regional meets, where she quickly stood out as a rising talent. Her routines were filled with an energy and joy that captivated audiences. While she still had much to learn technically, her performances were marked by an infectious spirit that resonated with both judges and spectators. Katelyn was not just another talented gymnast; she had an innate ability to connect with people through her performances, a quality that would later define her career.

Katelyn's early success in gymnastics also came with challenges. The demands of training and the need to balance school and family life required a level of commitment that many children her age struggled with. However, Katelyn approached these challenges with the same determination she showed on the mat. Her days were filled with practice sessions, schoolwork, and the normal activities of childhood, yet she managed to maintain a sense of balance through it all. Her family's support played a key role in helping her navigate these pressures, ensuring she never lost sight of the fun that first brought her to the sport.

As Katelyn continued to train and compete, she developed a deeper understanding of what gymnastics meant to her. It was no longer just an activity to burn off energy; it had become a central part of her identity. She thrived on the structure and discipline of training, finding purpose in pursuing perfection. Yet, what set Katelyn apart from many of her peers was her refusal to let the pressures of competition take away her enjoyment of the sport. Even as she began to compete at higher levels, she maintained the joyful, carefree approach that had characterized her earliest days in the gym.

Her love for gymnastics was evident in every routine she performed, a fact that did not escape her coaches. They noticed that Katelyn had a unique ability to bring personality into her performances, making her stand out even in a field filled with talented athletes. While many young gymnasts focused solely on executing their skills precisely, Katelyn infused her routines with a vitality that made her performances memorable. This ability to balance technical skill with emotional expression would later become one of her trademarks.

Despite the increasing demands of competitive gymnastics, Katelyn never lost her connection to the sport's lighter side. She was known for her playful attitude during training, often bringing a sense of fun to even the most grueling sessions. Her teammates were drawn to her positive energy, and her coaches appreciated her ability to keep things light while still working hard. This balance of discipline and joy became a defining feature of Katelyn's approach to gymnastics, carrying her through the highs and lows of her career.

As Katelyn's skills improved, she set her sights on higher goals. Competing at the national level became a realistic possibility, and her coaches started preparing her for the challenges ahead. Yet, through all the hard work and preparation, Katelyn remained grounded in her love for the sport. She understood that gymnastics was not just about winning or achieving perfect scores; it was about expressing herself through movement, pushing her physical and mental limits, and finding joy.

This early period in Katelyn Ohashi's life was crucial in shaping her future as a gymnast and a person. The passion she discovered in those early years in Seattle would carry her through the ups and downs of her career, providing a source of strength and motivation during even the most difficult moments. This unshakable love for gymnastics, combined with her family's and coaches' unwavering support, laid the foundation for her future success, both inside and outside the gym. Through it all, Katelyn never lost sight of the joy and freedom that gymnastics had given her from the beginning, a lesson that would ultimately guide her toward becoming a champion gymnast and an advocate for self-acceptance and empowerment.

Early Training and the Support of Her Family

Katelyn Ohashi's early training in gymnastics was an intense and formative period in her life. Her introduction to the sport came when she was brimming with energy and curiosity. While many children her age were still exploring various activities, Katelyn quickly found herself drawn to the challenging and dynamic world of gymnastics. It became apparent from her first few sessions that she had a natural aptitude for it, and even at a young age, she displayed remarkable coordination and strength. This raw talent, combined with an infectious enthusiasm, made her stand out among her peers. Her coaches noticed her physical abilities and willingness to learn, adapt, and push herself, traits that would become central to her identity as an athlete.

Her family played an essential role in supporting her during this period. From the outset, they recognized her passion for the sport and made every effort to nurture it. Her mother, in particular, was a key figure in shaping Katelyn's journey. Having a background in gymnastics, she understood the demands of the sport, both physically and mentally. This personal experience allowed her to guide Katelyn through the early stages of her training with a deep understanding of what it would take to succeed. Her mother was more than just a supportive parent; she was Katelyn's first coach and mentor, offering practical advice and emotional encouragement whenever challenges arose.

As Katelyn's training became more rigorous, her family adjusted their schedules to ensure she could pursue her passion without feeling overwhelmed. It wasn't uncommon for her mother to drive her long distances to attend specialized training sessions or competitions, all while balancing the needs of the rest of the family. These sacrifices were significant, but her family embraced them wholeheartedly, knowing how much gymnastics meant to Katelyn. This level of commitment from her family allowed her to focus on her development, knowing she had a reliable support system behind her.

Though not directly involved in gymnastics, Katelyn's father was a constant source of motivation. He attended her competitions, cheered her on, and provided a stable emotional foundation. His presence at events helped ease the pressure often accompanying young athletes as they began competing at higher levels. The presence of her siblings was also crucial. They were her biggest fans, attending her performances and offering encouragement during victories and setbacks. The tight-knit nature of her family created an environment where Katelyn felt secure, even when the pressures of training and competition began to mount.

Her coaches were also instrumental in these early years. Recognizing her potential, they worked diligently to refine her technique and build her strength. Gymnastics requires extraordinary discipline, and Katelyn's coaches were there to guide her through the demanding routines that would eventually make her a standout performer. Her ability to grasp new concepts quickly and apply corrections with precision impressed them. Her training sessions became more intense as her skill level increased, but Katelyn's love for the sport motivated her. Her coaches pushed her to the limits of her abilities while maintaining a nurturing approach, knowing how important it was for young gymnasts to remain excited about their sport.

One of the challenges Katelyn faced during this period was balancing the intensity of training with the joys of childhood. While many of her peers spent their free time playing or socializing, Katelyn was committed to perfecting her routines, often spending hours in the gym after school. Her schedule was rigorous, and there were moments when the physical and mental toll of training could have become overwhelming. Yet, she remained undeterred, largely because her family ensured she never lost sight of the fun that first drew her to gymnastics. They encouraged her to maintain friendships, enjoy time away from the gym, and remember that gymnastics was just one part of her life.

Her family's support extended beyond the practicalities of getting her to practices and competitions. They fostered an environment where Katelyn could express her ambitions and fears openly. This open communication helped her navigate the inevitable setbacks of elite training. Whether recovering from minor injuries, missing out on a win, or feeling the stress of high-stakes competitions, Katelyn knew she could rely on her family to provide comfort and perspective. This emotional backing was invaluable, as it allowed her to approach gymnastics with a healthy mindset, knowing she was loved and valued regardless of her performance.

With her deep understanding of the sport, Katelyn's mother became a key figure in navigating the more challenging aspects of her training. As Katelyn's routines grew more complex, requiring greater precision and strength, her mother helped her develop strategies to cope with both the physical and mental strain. Whether through words of wisdom or being present at her training sessions, her mother gave Katelyn the emotional grounding to stay focused. This level of involvement didn't mean constant oversight; rather, a steady presence reminded Katelyn she wasn't alone in her journey.

Katelyn's training during this period was intense, but it also brought out the best in her. She thrived on the challenge, often pushing herself beyond what was required. Her family recognized her extraordinary dedication and worked hard to ensure she remained physically and emotionally healthy. They understood that gymnastics while demanding, was a passion that gave her immense joy and a sense of purpose. This combination of family support and personal determination helped Katelyn through the grueling early years of training, setting the stage for her later successes.

As Katelyn moved through the ranks of competitive gymnastics, her family's role became even more important. The higher the level she competed at, the more intense the demands became. Travel for competitions increased, training sessions became longer, and the stakes grew. But through it all, her family remained her strongest supporter. They helped her manage the pressures of competition by creating a home environment where she could relax and recharge. This sense of balance was critical to Katelyn's ability to handle the increasing demands of the sport without losing her passion for it.

One of the remarkable things about Katelyn's early training was her ability to maintain a positive outlook even as the challenges grew. Much of this can be attributed to her strong support system at home. While her peers might have buckled under the weight of expectation, Katelyn continued approaching her sport with the same joy and enthusiasm she had from the start. Her family's unwavering encouragement allowed her to take risks, face setbacks, and keep striving toward her goals, knowing she had a network of people who believed in her no matter what.

The combination of early training and familial support created a foundation to sustain Katelyn throughout her gymnastics career. Her natural talent, combined with the guidance of her coaches and the love of her family, helped her navigate the ups and downs of the sport with resilience and determination. These formative years were about more than just developing the physical skills required to compete at the highest levels; they were about building the mental and emotional strength needed to persevere through the inevitable challenges. This balance of physical and emotional support is what allowed Katelyn to not only succeed in gymnastics but also to emerge as a confident and empowered individual.

The Path to Junior Elite Gymnastics

Katelyn Ohashi's journey toward junior elite gymnastics was marked by determination, talent, and a love for the sport that began to crystallize as she entered her first competition. From the moment she stepped into the world of competitive gymnastics, it was evident that she had both the technical skill and the mental fortitude necessary to excel. Her early years in the gym had laid a solid foundation, but competing against other gymnasts introduced new challenges. The atmosphere of competition brought out Katelyn's desire to perform her best and, in many ways, pushed her to achieve more than she had ever imagined. Her first few competitive gymnastics experiences would prove pivotal, setting the stage for her rise in the junior elite ranks.

The structure and rigor of the competition required her to hone her skills at a new level. While practice routines and training sessions were essential, performing in front of judges and spectators brought different pressures. This transition from practice to competition can be daunting for any young athlete, but Katelyn seemed to thrive on its excitement and challenge. The thrill of executing a routine in front of an audience gave her a sense of purpose and determination, igniting a competitive spirit that would drive her through the coming years. She enjoyed the spotlight, not just because of its attention but because it gave her a chance to prove what she could achieve.

Her first competitions were local meets, where she had the opportunity to test her abilities against other gymnasts in her region. These smaller events were crucial stepping stones in her development. Though the stakes were lower than national competitions, they allowed her to acclimate to the environment of competitive gymnastics. Each performance came with challenges, whether mastering the balance beam, executing a perfect floor routine, or sticking a landing after a vault. These early successes and setbacks in local competitions helped her build resilience and understand what it would take to progress.

Katelyn's first few competitions were marked by solid performances that began to attract attention. Though the competition was stiff, she stood out for her precision, grace, and the natural ease with which she performed complex routines. Even at a young age, she was able to combine technical difficulty with artistic expression, making her routines memorable. As she competed more frequently, her confidence grew and became increasingly comfortable under pressure. This ability to remain calm and focused, even in the face of fierce competition, would become one of her greatest strengths as she moved up the ranks.

As Katelyn continued to compete, her coaches recognized that she had the potential to succeed at a much higher level. They began preparing her for the transition to more elite competitions, focusing on refining her technique and increasing the difficulty of her routines. This period was one of intense growth for Katelyn. She was no longer just a talented young gymnast; she was beginning to emerge as a serious contender in the sport. The increased intensity of her training sessions reflected this shift, as her coaches pushed her to master more complex skills that would set her apart from her peers.

Her transition into the junior elite ranks required physical preparation and mental resilience. The pressure to succeed at higher-level competitions can be overwhelming, especially for young athletes, but Katelyn's ability to remain grounded helped her navigate this challenging phase of her career. Her family continued to be an unwavering source of support, providing her with the stability she needed to thrive. They encouraged her to maintain balance, reminding her that while gymnastics was important, it wasn't everything. This balance allowed Katelyn to stay motivated and focused without feeling the crushing weight of expectations.

Katelyn's breakthrough came when she began competing at the national level. Her performances at these larger competitions were nothing short of remarkable. She began to consistently place in the top ranks, gaining recognition from judges, her fellow gymnasts, and their coaches. Her routines were a combination of precision, strength, and artistry, and her ability to execute them with such fluidity made her a standout. As her reputation grew, so did the level of competition, but Katelyn welcomed the challenge. She had found her stride and was determined to prove she belonged among the best junior gymnasts in the country.

The increased exposure to elite-level competition came with its own set of challenges. The intensity of the training, the travel, and the constant pressure to perform at her best began to take their toll. But Katelyn's inner drive kept her going. She wasn't content just competing; she wanted to win, to push herself to achieve more with each competition. Her coaches, recognizing her potential, began tailoring her training to prepare her for the junior elite level. They increased the difficulty of her routines, focused on perfecting her form, and worked on building her endurance. Every competition became a stepping stone toward the next, with each victory reinforcing her belief in her abilities.

As Katelyn continued to rise through the ranks, she began to experience her first real taste of national success. Competing against some of the best young gymnasts in the country, she held her own, consistently finishing among the top performers. These victories were more than just medals or titles; they validated the countless hours she had spent training, refining her skills, and pushing herself beyond her limits. Each competition was a chance for her to showcase what she had worked so hard to achieve, and with every successful routine, she moved closer to her goal of becoming one of the top gymnasts in the country.

However, the path to junior elite gymnastics wasn't without its setbacks. Like any athlete, Katelyn faced moments of doubt and frustration. Injuries, missed opportunities, and the pressures of competition all weighed heavily on her at times. But through it all, she maintained a strong sense of purpose. She understood that these challenges were part of the process and that overcoming them would only strengthen her. Her family and coaches were always there to provide support and guidance, helping her navigate the ups and downs of competitive gymnastics.

Despite these challenges, Katelyn's commitment to her sport never wavered. She continued to push herself, driven by the desire to achieve her full potential. Her successes in the junior elite ranks were a testament to her hard work, dedication, and unwavering belief in herself. As she entered more prestigious competitions, her performances became increasingly polished, and her reputation as a rising star in the gymnastics world solidified. Her journey from those early local competitions to the junior elite level was one of determination and growth, both as an athlete and a person.

By the time Katelyn reached the junior elite level, she had already built an impressive resume of victories and accolades. But more importantly, she had developed the mental toughness and resilience needed to succeed at the highest levels of the sport. Her experiences in those early competitions prepared her for the challenges ahead, giving her the confidence and belief in herself to carry her through the rest of her gymnastics career. With each routine, each competition, and each victory, Katelyn Ohashi proved to herself and the world that she had what it took to compete at the highest level.

Chapter 2: Rising Through the Ranks

Competing at the Highest Level

As Katelyn Ohashi advanced in her gymnastics career, she found herself competing against some of the best young athletes in the country, many of whom would go on to become future Olympians. This stage of her journey brought new challenges but also introduced her to a higher level of competition that tested her skills and mental strength in ways she hadn't experienced before. Stepping onto the mat with athletes who had similar dreams of reaching the pinnacle of the sport pushed Katelyn to elevate her performance and sharpen her focus.

When she entered these elite competitions, Katelyn felt the weight of what was at stake. The intensity of the atmosphere, the precision required to succeed, and the knowledge that she was going head-to-head with future stars of gymnastics pushed her to give everything she had in every routine. This level demanded perfection, unlike earlier competitions, focusing on building skills and gaining experience. Each performance was an opportunity to rise to the occasion or fall short. Katelyn quickly realized that even the smallest mistake could be the difference between winning and losing.

Competing against athletes who would later represent their countries in the Olympics was inspiring and intimidating. Katelyn was surrounded by gymnasts whose dedication to the sport was unparalleled, and many of them had been training with Olympic aspirations from a young age. These competitors were not only physically gifted but also had a level of mental toughness that set them apart. The stakes were high, and the margin for error was razor-thin. Katelyn had to adjust to the fact that, at this level, there were no easy wins. Each victory had to be earned through precision, endurance, and consistency.

The presence of future Olympians in her competitions didn't just push Katelyn to perform better; it also reminded her of her goals. Watching these athletes compete, she saw firsthand what it took to excel at the highest level. The physical conditioning, the hours of practice, the mental resilience, these were all things Katelyn had been developing throughout her career. Still, she saw them on full display in the gymnasts around her. Competing against these athletes forced her to push herself physically and mentally harder to keep up with the increasing level of competition.

Both triumphs and setbacks marked Katelyn's rise to competing at the highest level. There were moments when she felt unstoppable, her routines executed with flawless precision and strength. But there were also times when the pressure seemed overwhelming, the competition felt too fierce, and doubts began to creep in. Facing athletes who were just as hungry for success as she was taught Katelyn valuable lessons about resilience and perseverance. During these competitions, she learned how to bounce back from a disappointing performance, shake off the weight of expectations, and stay focused on her long-term goals.

One of the defining aspects of Katelyn's journey at this level was the growing sense of camaraderie she developed with her fellow gymnasts. Although they were competing against each other, there was mutual respect and understanding among the athletes who had reached this elite stage. Many future Olympians she faced would become her teammates, friends, and mentors. These relationships added another layer to the competitive experience; Katelyn wasn't just competing against rivals; she was part of a community of gymnasts who understood the unique challenges of the sport.

Despite the intense competition, Katelyn continued to thrive. She refined her routines, working tirelessly with her coaches to perfect each element and increase the difficulty of her performances. The complexity of her routines grew as she mastered new skills, and her confidence soared as she consistently placed among the top competitors. Whenever she stepped onto the mat, Katelyn knew she could execute routines competing with the best. The drive to match the performances of future Olympians pushed her to elevate her gymnastics to a level she hadn't thought possible.

However, the physical demands of competing at such a high level began to take their toll. Katelyn experienced the aches and pains that come with years of rigorous training, and injuries became an ever-present risk. Gymnastics is an unforgiving sport; even minor injuries can seriously affect an athlete's career. As Katelyn pushed her body to new limits, she also had to learn how to listen to it, balancing her drive for success with avoiding burnout or long-term injury. This balance was critical, especially as the competition continued to intensify.

Amid these challenges, Katelyn's family remained a constant source of support. They had been with her since the beginning, and as the stakes grew higher, their encouragement and belief in her abilities helped her stay grounded. While the demands of elite gymnastics required Katelyn to spend most of her time training and competing, her family ensured she maintained a sense of normalcy outside the gym. This support system was essential for Katelyn as she navigated the pressures of competing against future Olympians, helping her stay focused and motivated even when the odds seemed stacked against her.

Katelyn's performances at this level caught the attention of coaches, judges, and fans alike. Her routines blend power, grace, and artistry, and her ability to deliver under pressure sets her apart from many competitors. She wasn't just competing; she was making a name for herself as one of the most promising young gymnasts in the sport. Each competition brought new opportunities to prove herself, and each victory reinforced her belief that she had what it took to compete with the best.

As she continued to rise through the ranks, Katelyn's ambitions of reaching the Olympics seemed closer than ever. She had proven she could hold her own against future Olympians, and her path was clear. But with success came increased pressure, both from external sources and from within. The expectations placed on Katelyn, whether from her coaches, fans, or herself, were immense. Yet she never let these expectations define her. Instead, she used them as fuel, pushing herself to improve with every routine, every competition, and every challenge.

Competing against future Olympians was a turning point in Katelyn's gymnastics career. It was a period of immense growth, both personally and athletically. These competitions tested her limits and showed her what was possible when she committed herself fully to her craft. While the path wasn't always easy, Katelyn's experiences at the highest level of competition shaped her into the athlete she would become, a gymnast known for her talent and her resilience, determination, and ability to rise to the occasion when it mattered most. Each moment on the mat was a testament to her hard work and her passion for the sport, and it was clear that her journey was far from over.

National Titles and International Recognition

As Katelyn Ohashi continued to build her career in gymnastics, the accolades began to pile up, marking her transition from a promising young athlete to a national sensation. Her journey to winning national titles resulted from years of dedication, and her rise in the competitive arena was inspiring and hard-earned. These victories were not just about medals; they were milestones that highlighted the skill, artistry, and determination that Katelyn brought to her performances. With each routine, she elevated her status, catching the eyes of coaches, judges, and fans alike.

Winning national titles was no small feat. The level of competition at these events was fierce, with gymnasts from across the country all vying for the top spot. Katelyn, however, had a unique ability to stand out. Her routines blended power, grace, and creativity, allowing her to impress the judges consistently. She approached each competition with meticulous attention to detail, ensuring that every element of her performance was polished. Her ability to easily perform difficult maneuvers and fluidity became one of her trademarks.

Katelyn's technical ability and ability to connect with the audience set her apart from her competitors. While gymnastics is often judged on precision and execution, Katelyn brought an extra artistry to her routines. Her expressive performances resonated with fans, making her dynamic floor routines iconic. The joy she displayed while competing was infectious, and it wasn't long before she became one of the most recognizable faces in U.S. gymnastics.

Her rise to national prominence wasn't without its challenges. The pressure to succeed on such a large stage could have been overwhelming for many athletes, but Katelyn thrived under it. She knew each competition was an opportunity to prove herself and embraced the chance to showcase her talents. There were moments of intense competition where the difference between first and second place came down to the smallest of details. Katelyn's focus and ability to deliver under pressure set her apart in these moments.

One of the defining moments in her career was when she captured her first major national title. This victory culminated years of training and sacrifice and began a new chapter in her career. With this win, Katelyn solidified her place among the best gymnasts in the country. It wasn't just the title itself that was significant; it was the message it sent. Katelyn had arrived and was a force to be reckoned with in the sport.

Her success on the national stage opened doors to international competitions, where Katelyn would face some of the best gymnasts from around the world. Competing internationally was a different kind of challenge. The routines were more complex, the competition even more intense, and the stakes higher. But Katelyn was ready for this new phase of her career. She knew that representing her country was both an honor and a responsibility, and she approached each international competition with the same passion and dedication that had carried her through her national victories.

Katelyn's performances on the international stage were met with admiration. Her routines displayed difficulty and execution, putting her in contention with the top gymnasts globally. She was no longer just a national star but gaining recognition on the world stage. Competing against international talent tested her abilities and showed her how far she had come. Each competition brought new challenges, but Katelyn's ability to adapt and rise to the occasion was a testament to her resilience.

Her international recognition wasn't limited to her competitive performances. Katelyn became known for her charisma, energy, and ability to bring something fresh to the sport. While many gymnasts focused purely on the technical aspects of their routines, Katelyn's routines celebrated movement and expression. Her international competitors respected her for the unique style she brought to the floor, and her presence at these events helped raise her profile even further.

The transition from competing nationally to competing on the international stage also required adjustments in training. Katelyn worked closely with her coaches to refine her routines, adding new elements and increasing the difficulty to match international competition standards. These adjustments were not always easy, but Katelyn was determined to keep pushing herself to new heights. The hard work paid off, as her international performances consistently earned her high scores and praise from judges.

One of the key moments in Katelyn's international career was her participation in a major global competition, where she delivered a flawless routine that garnered significant attention. The performance perfectly blended technical skill and artistry, earning her one of the event's highest scores. This routine secured her a podium finish and solidified her status as a gymnast to watch on the global stage. The routine reflected all the years of hard work, showcasing her ability to compete at the highest level.

Katelyn's rise to international recognition also came with new opportunities. She was invited to compete in exhibitions and participate in global tours, where she could perform in front of audiences worldwide. These opportunities allowed her to experience gymnastics' global reach and inspire fans in different countries. For Katelyn, it was not just about the competition but about sharing her love of the sport with others and using her platform to make an impact.

While her national titles and international recognition were significant accomplishments, Katelyn never lost sight of the values that had driven her to success in the first place. She remained grounded, always remembering the support of her family and coaches, who had been with her every step of the way. Despite the fame and recognition that came with her achievements, Katelyn continued to approach her training and competitions with humility and a deep respect for the sport.

Her journey to the top was not just a story of success; it was a story of resilience, perseverance, and a deep passion for gymnastics. The national titles and international recognition were important milestones, but for Katelyn, they were just part of a larger journey. Each competition, each routine, and each victory brought her closer to her personal goals and solidified her place in the sport's history. Through her success, Katelyn became a role model for young gymnasts worldwide, showing them that anything was possible with hard work, dedication, and a love for the sport.

The Burden of Expectations

As Katelyn Ohashi's career gained momentum, the expectations placed upon her began to grow exponentially. Like many sports, gymnastic success comes with a unique set of pressures beyond the physical demands of training and competition. For Katelyn, the weight of these expectations intensified as she rose through the ranks, evolving from a talented young gymnast into one of the sport's brightest stars. With each accolade, the pressure to maintain her performance level and continue winning became a constant presence in her life, shaping her personal and professional experiences.

From an early age, Katelyn was recognized for her potential. Coaches, peers, and the gymnastics community saw a rare combination of grace, power, and determination in her. This attention, though well-meaning, created a sense of expectation that became increasingly difficult to manage. Every achievement came with a demand for more, more difficult routines, higher scores, and greater success. The joy initially fueled her love for gymnastics and began to shift under the burden of needing to meet the standards that others had set for her.

The pressure was not only external. Like many athletes, Katelyn's inner drive pushed her to be the best. This self-imposed demand for excellence made her approach every competition with an intensity that sometimes bordered on perfectionism. She scrutinized every routine, every movement, knowing that even the slightest mistake could mean the difference between winning and losing. The gymnastics world is unforgiving in its pursuit of perfection, and Katelyn internalized this, holding herself to impossible standards. The fear of failure, of letting down those who believed in her, began to weigh heavily on her mind.

One of the key sources of this pressure was the expectation that Katelyn would follow the well-worn path of other top gymnasts, competing at the highest level and potentially aiming for Olympic glory. The dream of the Olympics is one that many young gymnasts share, and for Katelyn, this dream was very much within reach. However, the closer she got to this goal, the more the pressure mounted. Every competition and every practice session became a test of whether she was still on track for this pinnacle achievement. The stakes were high, and the constant comparisons to other gymnasts who had achieved Olympic success added to the already immense burden.

The media also played a significant role in amplifying these pressures. As Katelyn's profile grew, so did the attention from reporters and commentators. Her performances were dissected, and her potential was a frequent topic of discussion. While the attention brought her recognition, it also had a darker side. The scrutiny she faced was often relentless, with every mistake magnified and every victory carrying the expectation of more. This constant analysis became a part of her everyday life, and the pressure to live up to the public's perception of her abilities became almost suffocating.

For Katelyn, the physical demands of gymnastics also contributed to the pressure she felt. The sport is one of the most demanding in the world, requiring athletes to train rigorously for years to perfect their routines. Injuries are common, and gymnastics' toll on the body is immense. As Katelyn advanced in her career, she began to experience the wear and tear that comes with years of pushing her body to its limits. The expectation to continue performing at a high level despite these challenges became another source of stress. She knew that taking time to recover or pulling back from competition could be a sign of weakness, adding another layer of complexity to the overwhelming pressure to succeed.

Despite her successes, Katelyn also faced moments of doubt and uncertainty, which were often exacerbated by the expectations that surrounded her. The fear of not living up to the hype and not meeting the standards set for her created an emotional strain that was difficult to manage. The constant drive for perfection left little room for error, and Katelyn often grappled with feelings of inadequacy, even when she was at the top of her game. The pursuit of excellence, while motivating, also became a source of mental exhaustion.

The competitive nature of gymnastics meant that Katelyn was always aware of the other athletes striving for the same goals. The sport is inherently comparative, with scores, rankings, and titles as the measure of success. This environment fostered a sense of competition beyond the gym, as Katelyn constantly felt the need to prove herself to others and herself. The desire to outperform her peers and be the best was a driving force, but it also added to her weight. Each competition tested her physical abilities and her ability to meet the ever-growing expectations placed upon her.

Family and friends provided a support system, but even this support could sometimes contribute to Katelyn's pressure. Her loved ones wanted to see her succeed, and while they offered encouragement and reassurance, Katelyn always wanted to not let them down. Their sacrifices to support her career were not lost on her, and this knowledge sometimes made the burden even heavier. The fear of disappointing those who had invested so much in her journey became another aspect of the pressure she faced.

As Katelyn's career progressed, she also began to experience the pressures associated with maintaining her public image. Gymnasts, like many athletes, are often seen as role models, and there was an expectation that Katelyn would embody this image both on and off the mat. The desire to live up to the ideals that others projected onto her added to the already intense scrutiny she faced. This pressure to always present herself in a certain way, to be a perfect representation of the sport, was yet another layer of expectation that weighed on her shoulders.

The constant need to perform, win, and meet the expectations of coaches, fans, and herself sometimes became overwhelming. Katelyn began to realize that the very thing she had once loved, gymnastics, was now the source of her greatest stress. The pressure to succeed often overshadowed the joy of competing and expressing herself through her routines. Each competition brought the anxiety of needing to prove herself again, and the cumulative effect of this pressure began to take a toll on her mental and physical well-being. Katelyn's journey through the world of gymnastics was marked by tremendous success, but it was also shaped by the immense pressure to meet the expectations that came with that success. The weight of these expectations, from external sources and from within, created a complex dynamic that influenced every aspect of her career. While she continued to push forward, the burden of always having to perform at the highest level became a defining feature of her experience as an elite gymnast. Despite the challenges, Katelyn's resilience and determination remained constant, even as she navigated the difficult balance between the sport's joy and the pressures accompanying it.

Chapter 3: Injuries and Setbacks

A Promising Career Halted by Injury

Katelyn Ohashi's career was full of promise and excitement, but as with many elite athletes, injury became a defining moment in her journey. The nature of gymnastics, with its intense physical demands, meant that every performance came with the risk of physical harm. As her skills evolved and her routines grew more complex, the strain on her body increased. Over time, the toll of years of rigorous training began to manifest in various ways. What had once been a source of joy and personal expression turned into a battle between her body and her aspirations, as injury threatened to derail everything she had worked for.

The first signs of trouble came subtly. Gymnastics is a sport that demands constant training, often for hours each day, and the repetition of difficult skills can put enormous stress on an athlete's muscles, joints, and bones. Katelyn's routines were known for their power and grace, but behind the elegance was an unrelenting physical grind. For years, she pushed herself to perfect each movement, each twist and turn. But with that dedication came inevitable wear and tear. She began to notice small aches and pains, minor injuries that initially seemed manageable.

For an athlete of Katelyn's caliber, pushing through pain was part of the process. She had developed a mental toughness that allowed her to work through discomfort, knowing that temporary pain was often a stepping stone to achieving something greater. However, as the intensity of her training increased, so did the frequency and severity of her injuries. What started as manageable discomfort soon turned into something more serious. Katelyn's body was signaling that it was reaching its limit. Still, the pressure to continue performing and meet the expectations of coaches, fans, and herself made it difficult to fully address these issues.

One of the defining aspects of Katelyn's injuries was their cumulative effect. Unlike a single catastrophic incident, her body was breaking down slowly over time. The constant pounding her joints and muscles endured particularly her back and shoulders, began to take a serious toll. Her once-flawless execution of high-difficulty routines started to feel strained, and the pain she had once been able to push through became more intense. Her body could no longer recover as quickly as it once had, and the toll of years of high-impact training began to catch up with her.

The mental impact of dealing with injury cannot be underestimated. For Katelyn, it was not just a physical battle but also a psychological one. She had spent years building her identity around gymnastics, dedicating her life to pursuing sports excellence. To suddenly face the possibility that her body might not be able to keep up with her dreams was a devastating realization. The thought of being sidelined and unable to compete at the level she knew she was capable of weighed heavily on her. She began to confront the reality that her body might not allow her to continue pushing toward the goals she had set for herself.

Gymnasts are known for their resilience, and Katelyn was no different. She tried to manage her injuries through physical therapy, rest, and modified training. There were periods when she believed she could recover fully and return to her peak form. But the reality of her situation became increasingly clear: the injuries were not going away. The pain persisted, and despite her best efforts, her body was no longer able to withstand the demands of elite gymnastics. Each time she stepped onto the mat, there was the looming fear that another misstep or wrong landing could lead to further damage.

The decision to address her injuries seriously did not come easily. Like many athletes, Katelyn had learned to equate pain with progress. She had pushed through difficult moments before, and accepting that this time might be different was hard. But the physical toll had reached a point where ignoring it was no longer an option. Her back, in particular, had become a constant source of pain, and she knew that continuing to train at the level required for elite competition could result in long-term damage. The thought of permanently injuring herself, losing her mobility, or being unable to live a healthy life outside of gymnastics began to weigh on her decision-making.

The emotional aspect of dealing with injury was perhaps the most difficult part for Katelyn. Gymnastics had been her life for as long as she could remember, and stepping back from the sport felt like giving up a part of herself. The idea of not being able to compete, of not being able to do the thing she loved most, was heartbreaking. She had spent years working toward specific goals, and now it felt like those dreams were slipping away. The frustration of feeling held back by her own body was immense, and it took time for her to come to terms with the reality of her situation.

Her family and coaches provided support during this difficult time, but even their encouragement could not erase the sense of loss she felt. Gymnastics had always been a source of joy and pride for Katelyn, and now it had become a source of physical and emotional pain. She was forced to confront the idea that her career, which had once seemed so full of promise, might be ending far earlier than she had imagined. The future, which had once been filled with dreams of Olympic competition and further success, was now uncertain.

Despite the challenges, Katelyn's resilience began to show itself in a new way. While her injuries forced her to step back from the intense training and competition that had defined her life, they also allowed her to reflect on what she wanted from her future. She realized that gymnastics, while incredibly important to her, was not the only thing that defined her. The experience of dealing with injury taught her about her strength, both mentally and physically, and helped her develop a new perspective on her career and life outside of the sport.

Stepping away from elite gymnastics allowed Katelyn to focus on healing her body and mind. She began to prioritize her health, understanding that pushing herself to the point of further injury was not the path she wanted to take. Instead of seeing her injuries as a defeat, she began to view them as an opportunity for growth. The time away from competition allowed her to explore other interests and passions, and she started to think about how she could use her platform to inspire others beyond the gymnastics world.

The injury that had once seemed like the end of her dreams became a turning point in Katelyn's life. It forced her to reevaluate her priorities and think about what truly mattered. While she had to let go of certain aspects of her gymnastics career, she gained a new sense of purpose and direction. The lessons she learned from dealing with injury, patience, perseverance, and self-acceptance became central to her moving forward. Although her career was altered, Katelyn's story was far from over. She emerged from this challenging period with a renewed sense of identity and a determination to impact in ways she hadn't imagined.

Dealing with Pain, Recovery, and the Reality of Missing the Olympics

As Katelyn Ohashi faced the harsh reality of missing the Olympics, a dream she had nurtured since childhood, she was forced to confront not only the physical pain of her injuries but also the emotional weight of unfulfilled expectations. The path to recovery for an elite gymnast is rarely straightforward, and for Katelyn, it became a deeply personal journey filled with disappointment, resilience, and self-discovery. The years she had dedicated to gymnastics, training countless hours and pushing her body to its limits, now seemed to stand still. What had once been a clear trajectory toward the highest stage in sports had transformed into a complex battle between her body's limitations and her inner desire to continue.

The physical pain that Katelyn endured was intense and constant. Her body had been subjected to years of grueling routines, with each twist, flip, and landing taking its toll on her joints, muscles, and bones. Gymnastics is a sport that demands extreme flexibility and strength, and the strain on her body became more evident as she advanced in her career. Despite her immense talent and passion, Katelyn could not escape the reality that her body was breaking down. Back pain had become a regular companion, and it was no longer something she could simply push through. Her shoulders and wrists also bore the brunt of repetitive movements, leading to chronic discomfort and the kind of injuries that, once accumulated, became harder to overcome.

Doctors and therapists worked tirelessly to help her manage the pain, but recovery was slow and often frustrating. Physical therapy sessions were grueling, and while Katelyn was determined to heal, the process was far from linear. Some days felt like progress, where she could see a glimpse of her old self, capable of performing the skills she had mastered over the years. But other days, the pain would flare up, reminding her of the fragility of her situation. The mental toll of this back-and-forth battle was just as significant as the physical struggle. For someone whose life had revolved around pushing through challenges, the realization that her body might not cooperate with her ambitions was difficult to accept.

What made the pain even harder to bear was the looming sense of what she was missing. Katelyn was sidelined as her peers continued to compete, some of whom were on their way to becoming Olympians. It was heartbreaking to see them succeed, knowing she could no longer compete at that level. The Olympics had always been a goal; missing out on that opportunity left her with a deep sense of loss. She had once stood shoulder to shoulder with athletes who would go on to represent their countries on the world's biggest stage, and now, her place among them seemed to have vanished. The emotional strain of this realization weighed heavily on her as she tried to balance recovery with the recognition that her Olympic dreams were slipping away.

Yet, through the pain and disappointment, Katelyn grappled with more than just her Olympic aspirations. She began to question her identity as a gymnast, and what it meant to succeed outside the narrow framework she had once envisioned. For so long, her self-worth had been tied to her performance and potential in gymnastics. As her body forced her to step back, she was left to consider who she was without the promise of an Olympic future. This introspection, though challenging, would ultimately shape her perspective on life beyond the sport. During these difficult moments of reflection, she understood that her athletic achievements did not solely define her value.

Katelyn's support system, particularly her family, was essential during this period. Their unwavering encouragement allowed her to face the reality of her situation without feeling completely isolated. Her parents had always been a steady source of strength, and now, as she dealt with the pain and uncertainty of her injuries, they were there to remind her of the importance of her well-being. They encouraged her to prioritize recovery and to look beyond gymnastics, helping her realize that life's worth wasn't dependent on a single goal, no matter how grand. Their love and understanding gave her the space to heal, not just physically but emotionally as well.

As her body slowly healed, Katelyn had to accept that missing the Olympics wasn't a failure but a redirection. She began to explore other passions and interests that had been sidelined during her intense focus on gymnastics. Writing, art, and public speaking became outlets where she could express herself. These new avenues of creativity gave her a sense of fulfillment that helped counterbalance her loss from no longer competing at the highest level. The world outside the gym began expanding, and she realized she had more to offer than just her athletic talent.

The journey toward recovery also brought Katelyn face to face with the realities of mental health, something that had often been pushed aside in favor of physical performance. She learned that the mind, like the body, needs care and attention. Through therapy and introspection, she began to address the pressure she had placed on herself over the years. The constant need to perform, to be perfect, had taken a toll on her emotional well-being, and now, as she dealt with injury, she recognized the importance of mental balance. The process of healing her body became intertwined with the need to heal her mind, and this holistic approach to recovery allowed her to move forward in a healthier, more sustainable way.

The reality of missing the Olympics was painful, but it also allowed Katelyn to redefine what success meant to her. She had spent so many years chasing a singular goal, but now she realized there were other ways to make an impact. As she emerged from this period of reflection and healing, Katelyn became more outspoken about the importance of mental health and self-worth, using her platform to inspire others facing similar struggles. Her message evolved from purely athletic achievement to emphasizing the importance of balance, self-care, and resilience.

By confronting the pain and disappointment of missing the Olympics, Katelyn better understood herself and what truly mattered. She realized that while her gymnastics career had been an important part of her life, it was not the only thing that defined her. Though difficult, the experience of injury and recovery allowed her to grow in ways she hadn't anticipated. It allowed her to reassess her values and focus on what brought her true fulfillment. Through this journey, Katelyn emerged stronger as an athlete and an individual with a renewed sense of purpose and direction. She became a voice for others navigating similar challenges, using her story to encourage people to prioritize their physical and mental health and find meaning in their journey, regardless of their obstacles.

Reflecting on the Mental and Physical Toll of Elite Gymnastics

Katelyn Ohashi's journey through elite gymnastics reflected the immense joy of mastering a sport and the profound physical and mental toll that such a high level of commitment can exact. While her performances dazzled audiences and earned her recognition, the reality behind the scenes was far more complex. Elite gymnastics, though visually graceful, is an unforgiving pursuit. It demands discipline, sacrifice, and resilience, pushing athletes to their absolute limits. For Katelyn, years of grueling training sessions, constant pressure to excel, and the relentless pursuit of perfection left an indelible mark on her mentally and physically.

The physical toll of elite gymnastics is perhaps the most immediately apparent. From a young age, Katelyn's body was put through intense routines, repeatedly subjecting her muscles and joints to the high-impact nature of the sport. Gymnasts at her level are often expected to perform movements that require incredible strength, balance, and flexibility, but these moves also come with risks. The constant pounding on hard surfaces, combined with repetitive stress on certain parts of the body, creates an environment where injuries are almost inevitable. For Katelyn, the years of perfecting her skills led to numerous injuries, some of which lingered long after the immediate pain had faded.

The training regimen of an elite gymnast like Katelyn is unrelenting. Six or seven days a week were spent in the gym, sometimes for hours, working on routines that needed to be executed flawlessly. The intensity of this training took its toll on her physically. Stress fractures, muscle strains, and joint pain became part of her reality, and recovery was often rushed to ensure she could continue competing. As with many gymnasts, the pressure to push through injuries was ever-present. Coaches, teammates, and her drive to succeed created an atmosphere where resting was seen as a setback rather than a necessary component of long-term health.

Yet, while the physical toll of the sport was significant, the mental strain was just as profound. From the outside, gymnastics may appear to be all about physical prowess, but it is a sport that is equally demanding on the mind. The precision required in each movement means that any slip in focus can lead to errors, which, at the elite level, can result in devastating consequences. This need for constant concentration and the pressure to perform created an intense mental burden for Katelyn. The weight of expectations – both from others and herself – was ever-present. Her performances were scrutinized by coaches, judges, audiences, and even the media, adding layers of pressure to each competition.

For Katelyn, the mental strain was compounded by the expectations placed on her at a young age. As a gymnast who showed exceptional talent early on, eyes always watched her progress. With every successful competition, the expectations only grew. Coaches expected more from her, the gymnastics community anticipated greater achievements, and she, in turn, internalized these pressures. The weight of these expectations began to affect her mental health. The constant need to prove herself, to live up to the potential others saw in her, became exhausting. As the pressure to maintain perfection mounted, it eroded her sense of self-worth, making her feel her value was tied exclusively to her performances.

The pressure to maintain a certain body image was another factor that took a significant mental toll. Gymnastics, as a sport, places a heavy emphasis on aesthetics, and athletes are often judged not only on their skills but on how they look while performing. This focus on appearance led to unhealthy body standards within the sport, and Katelyn was no exception to this scrutiny. She faced criticism about her body, with comments from coaches and others in the gymnastics world about her weight and shape. This constant focus on her appearance, rather than her abilities, created deep insecurities and contributed to her struggles with body image. The mental strain of trying to fit into a mold imposed on her only intensified the overall toll of the sport.

These physical and mental burdens began manifesting in ways that affected her love for gymnastics. What had once been a source of joy and pride started to feel more like a weight she was carrying. The constant cycle of training, competing, recovering from injuries, and dealing with the pressure to succeed began to wear her down. Katelyn's body was signaling that it could no longer keep up with the demands of elite gymnastics, but her mind was also reaching a breaking point. The passion that had fueled her drive to succeed was overshadowed by the toll the sport took on her well-being.

Eventually, Katelyn realized that continuing down this path was unsustainable. Her mental health, which had been neglected in favor of physical performance, could no longer be ignored. The intense pressure she had placed on herself and the expectations from those around her had led to burnout. During this period, Katelyn began to step back and reflect on the broader impact that elite gymnastics had on her life. She started to see how the sport had shaped her – positively and negatively – and understood the importance of balance.

One of the hardest parts of this reflection was coming to terms with her sacrifices for the sport. From a young age, gymnastics had consumed much of her life. Time with friends and family, typical childhood experiences, and her education were often secondary to her training. The sport had shaped not only her body but her entire worldview. As she faced the reality of burnout, Katelyn had to grapple with the question of what life looked like outside of gymnastics. The intense physical and mental toll of the sport had forced her to reconsider her priorities and find ways to heal.

In the healing process, Katelyn began to rediscover herself outside the confines of elite gymnastics. She found new ways to channel her passion, using her platform to speak out about her challenges. Her openness about the mental and physical toll of the sport resonated with many, particularly younger gymnasts dealing with similar pressures. By sharing her story, Katelyn began her healing process and helped others understand that the pursuit of excellence should not come at the expense of one's well-being.

Through this reflection, Katelyn also came to appreciate the importance of mental health in athletics. The sport of gymnastics, like many others, often prioritizes physical performance while neglecting the mental health of its athletes. Katelyn's experience highlighted the need for a more holistic approach to training that values the athlete as a whole person, not just as a performer. Her journey became a powerful reminder that success in sports should not come at the cost of an athlete's mental and physical health.

Katelyn's reflection on the toll of elite gymnastics ultimately led to a broader understanding of what it means to succeed. She realized that true success is not just about winning medals or achieving perfection in a routine. It is about finding balance, maintaining health, and preserving one's sense of self. This realization marked a turning point in her life, where she began prioritizing her well-being over the demands of the sport. Through this journey, Katelyn emerged stronger, not just as an athlete but as an advocate for mental health and self-care in the world of sports.

Chapter 4: A New Beginning

Transitioning to Collegiate Gymnastics

Transitioning from elite gymnastics to collegiate competition brought a major shift in Katelyn Ohashi's life as an athlete and a person. The move to join the UCLA Bruins marked a turning point where she could continue pursuing her passion and redefine her relationship with the sport. After years of competing at the highest level and enduring the intense physical and emotional demands of elite gymnastics, this new chapter provided an opportunity to reconnect with the joy that initially drew her to gymnastics. At UCLA, Katelyn found a supportive environment that encouraged her to explore her talents in ways that were more aligned with her well-being.

The decision to attend UCLA and compete for their gymnastics team was not just about continuing her career; it was about seeking balance. While still competitive and demanding, collegiate gymnastics offered a different atmosphere than the elite level, centered around teamwork, camaraderie, and, most importantly, fun. After years of facing extreme pressure to perform flawlessly and dealing with the expectations of Olympic success, this new approach was refreshing. Katelyn embraced the opportunity to be part of a team that valued her for more than just her performance scores. For the first time in years, she could focus on enjoying gymnastics without feeling the weight of her earlier experiences.

Joining the UCLA Bruins, Katelyn was welcomed into one of the country's most prestigious collegiate gymnastics programs. UCLA's gymnastics team had a rich history of success, and its coaching staff, led by Valorie Kondos Field, had created a culture that was not only about winning but about fostering personal growth and empowerment. "Miss Val," as the head coach was affectionately known, played a key role in helping Katelyn navigate this transition. Miss Val's coaching philosophy was grounded in the belief that gymnastics should be a tool for building character, confidence, and self-expression, not just for achieving medals. This approach resonated deeply with Katelyn, who had experienced the more cutthroat side of the sport at the elite level. Under Miss Val's guidance, Katelyn began to heal emotionally from the years of pressure and injury, and she started to see gymnastics as a source of joy again.

One of the most significant aspects of Katelyn's experience at UCLA was the shift from individual competition to team dynamics. At the elite level, the focus was often on individual performances, where gymnasts were judged primarily on their scores. Collegiate gymnastics, by contrast, strongly emphasized the team as a whole, with individual routines contributing to the team's overall score. This change allowed Katelyn to experience the sport in a more collaborative and supportive environment. Rather than feeling isolated by the pressure to be perfect, she was surrounded by teammates who cheered her on, celebrated her successes, and lifted her during difficult moments. The bonds she formed with her teammates became a source of strength and motivation, transforming her approach to the sport.

At UCLA, Katelyn's routines began to reflect her personality and creativity more than ever before. In collegiate gymnastics, athletes are given more freedom to express themselves through their floor routines, and Katelyn took full advantage of this. Her routines became not just exercises in athletic skill but performances that showcased her unique style and charisma. The iconic floor routine that eventually went viral, earning her a 10, was a perfect example of how Katelyn embraced this new phase of her gymnastics career. It was filled with energy, artistry, and joy, capturing the hearts of audiences not just because of its technical difficulty but because of the vitality with which she performed it.

While transitioning to collegiate gymnastics was a positive experience for Katelyn, it did not come without challenges. The physical toll that years of elite gymnastics had taken on her body remains. Injuries, particularly the chronic pain she experienced from previous issues, remained an obstacle that she had to manage. However, the UCLA training staff and coaches were attentive to her needs, prioritizing her long-term health over immediate results. This emphasis on care and recovery starkly contrasted with what she had experienced at the elite level, where gymnasts often felt pressure to push through pain for the sake of competition. At UCLA, Katelyn learned to listen to her body and take the necessary time to heal, allowing her to continue competing without risking further injury.

Mentally, the transition was also a time of growth and self-discovery. For years, Katelyn had been defined by her pursuit of Olympic glory, a goal that, while prestigious, had come with immense pressure. Stepping away from that path allowed her to redefine what success meant to her. Rather than being driven solely by the need to win or achieve perfection, Katelyn began to focus on personal fulfillment. She realized that success could be measured in terms of happiness, balance, and self-expression, not just scores or accolades. This shift in mindset helped her rebuild her confidence, which had been eroded by the intense scrutiny she had faced earlier in her career.

UCLA also provided Katelyn with an environment in which to explore her identity beyond gymnastics. The university's diverse and vibrant community encouraged her to engage in interests outside the sport, helping her develop a more well-rounded sense of self. As she pursued her academic studies and became involved in other campus activities, Katelyn started to see herself as more than just an athlete. This broader perspective was crucial in her journey toward self-acceptance and body positivity, which later became central themes in her advocacy work.

Katelyn's support from her family remained a constant source of strength throughout this transition. Her family had been by her side through the highs and lows of her gymnastics career, and their encouragement helped her navigate the new challenges she faced in college. Knowing she had a solid support system allowed Katelyn to take risks, try new things, and fully embrace the opportunities that UCLA offered. Her family's unwavering belief in her abilities as a gymnast and person was instrumental in her continued growth and success.

As Katelyn's time at UCLA progressed, she became a role model for her gymnastics prowess, resilience, and authenticity. Her journey resonated with many who had experienced similar pressures in their own lives, whether in sports or other areas. By embracing her individuality and rejecting the narrow standards of perfection that had once dictated her life, Katelyn inspired others to do the same. Her success at UCLA was not just about winning championships or earning perfect scores; it was about reclaiming and using her voice to advocate for positive change within the sport and beyond.

The transition to collegiate gymnastics allowed Katelyn to rediscover her love for the sport on her terms. It was a period of healing, growth, and self-discovery where she could reconcile the demands of gymnastics with her well-being. Through this experience, Katelyn was confident about expressing herself more freely in her routines and personal life. Her time with the UCLA Bruins became a defining chapter in her journey, shaping her athletic career and identity as an advocate for body positivity and mental health.

Coach Valorie Kondos Field's Influence

Valorie Kondos Field, affectionately known as "Miss Val," played an instrumental role in Katelyn Ohashi's transformation during her collegiate gymnastics career at UCLA. Having coached the UCLA

Bruins to multiple national championships, Miss Val was well-known for her technical expertise and her unique coaching philosophy, prioritizing her athletes' personal growth and well-being over winning at all costs. This holistic approach would become crucial in Katelyn's journey, helping her rebuild her confidence and rediscover the joy in gymnastics after years of physical and emotional strain from elite competition.

From their first interactions, Miss Val saw something that went beyond her gymnastics ability in Katelyn. She recognized the toll that competing at the elite level had taken on Katelyn, both physically and mentally. Years of being in the spotlight, grappling with injuries, and navigating the intense pressures of pursuing Olympic aspirations had left Katelyn with deep emotional scars. Miss Val brought to Katelyn's life the chance to reset and view the sport she loved from a new perspective that valued expression and enjoyment as much as excellence. This shift in focus was exactly what Katelyn needed to begin healing.

Miss Val's coaching style was vastly different from the intense and rigid environments Katelyn had experienced as a junior elite gymnast. Whereas elite coaches often focused narrowly on skill perfection and winning, Miss Val approached each athlete as a whole person, not just a gymnast. She believed the lessons learned in gymnastics could carry over into life, teaching resilience, discipline, and self-awareness. Miss Val's influence on Katelyn was profound, as she encouraged her to reconnect with the deeper reasons why she started gymnastics in the first place, her love for the sport, and her joy in performing.

Katelyn's initial experience under Miss Val's guidance was one of rebuilding. After facing the harsh realities of elite gymnastics, including criticism about her body and relentless pressure to meet impossible standards, she arrived at UCLA feeling both physically and emotionally depleted. Miss Val, however, reassured Katelyn that she had nothing to prove. She urged her to let go of the external pressures that had defined her gymnastics career for so long and instead focus on finding fulfillment in her routines. This message resonated deeply with Katelyn, who is tired of chasing perfection and ready to explore a different path.

As Katelyn settled into her new environment, Miss Val worked closely with her to nurture her confidence. One of the key ways she did this was by encouraging Katelyn to express herself freely in her floor routines. Miss Val's philosophy allowed her gymnasts to incorporate their personalities and creativity into their performances, giving them more freedom than they had previously experienced. For Katelyn, this was a revelation. She had spent years refining her technical skills, but now she was being asked to showcase her individuality and have fun in her performances. This shift allowed Katelyn to rediscover her love for performing, buried beneath years of competitive stress.

The floor routine that eventually went viral and earned Katelyn widespread recognition was the culmination of Miss Val's coaching philosophy. The routine displayed athletic ability and a joyful celebration of Katelyn's personality and spirit. It embodied the freedom and vitality that Miss Val had worked to instill in her gymnasts. Through that routine, Katelyn could share her authentic self with the world, a far cry from the rigid and controlled performances that had characterized her elite career. Miss Val's influence was evident in every move, as Katelyn performed with a sense of liberation that had been missing for much of her gymnastics journey.

But Miss Val's impact on Katelyn went beyond the routines. She also fostered a sense of self-acceptance and confidence in Katelyn, extending far beyond the gym. Miss Val was known for being a mentor who encouraged her athletes to embrace who they were and their flaws. She often spoke about the importance of self-love and mental well-being, advocating for an approach to gymnastics grounded in positivity and resilience. This was a vital message for

Katelyn, who had faced body shaming and immense pressure throughout her career. Miss Val taught her to see herself not as a product of her scores or appearance but as a strong and capable individual with the power to define her success.

Throughout her time at UCLA, Miss Val continued to provide Katelyn with the support and guidance she needed to grow as an athlete and a person. She helped her understand that setbacks, whether injuries or missed opportunities, did not define her worth. Instead, Miss Val framed these challenges as learning experiences, opportunities for Katelyn to build resilience and develop a healthier relationship with gymnastics. This mindset shift was crucial for Katelyn as she worked through the lingering effects of her past injuries and the mental strain of her elite career.

Miss Val's influence also extended to helping Katelyn understand the importance of self-care. Unlike the grueling pace of elite gymnastics, where athletes were often expected to push through pain and injury, Miss Val prioritized the long-term well-being of her gymnasts. She emphasized the need for rest, recovery, and balance, encouraging Katelyn to listen to her body and take time to heal when necessary. This approach starkly contrasted with what Katelyn had experienced in her early years, allowing her to approach gymnastics more sustainably. She no longer felt the need to push her body beyond its limits in the pursuit of perfection.

Under Miss Val's mentorship, Katelyn also began to explore her role as a leader on the team. Miss Val encouraged her to use her experiences to help uplift and support her teammates, many of whom looked up to her as a role model. Katelyn's journey from an elite gymnast to a collegiate athlete who prioritized joy and authenticity inspired those around her. She became a source of encouragement and strength for her teammates, embodying the values Miss Val instilled in the program. This sense of community and mutual support was a hallmark of Miss Val's coaching, and it played a significant role in Katelyn's growth as an athlete and an individual.

As Katelyn's confidence continued to grow, so did her influence beyond the world of gymnastics. Miss Val's encouragement to embrace her true self empowered Katelyn to speak out on issues that mattered to her, particularly around body positivity and mental health. Katelyn's experiences with body shaming and the pressures of elite gymnastics had given her a unique perspective. Under Miss Val's guidance, she felt encouraged to use her platform to advocate for positive change. Miss Val had taught her that her voice mattered, and Katelyn took this lesson to heart, using her story to inspire others who had faced similar struggles.

The relationship between Katelyn and Miss Val was one of trust, mutual respect, and empowerment. Miss Val saw Katelyn's potential as a gymnast and a whole person, and she worked tirelessly to help her realize that potential. Through their collaboration, Katelyn rebuilt her confidence, healed from the pressures of her elite career, and rediscovered the joy of gymnastics. More importantly, she learned to value herself for who she was, not just for what she could achieve. This profound influence shaped Katelyn's journey and continues to resonate in her life long after her time at UCLA.

Balancing School, Training, and Life Beyond Gymnastics

Balancing the demands of school, training, and life beyond gymnastics is no small feat for any collegiate athlete. This balancing act became crucial to her journey at UCLA for Katelyn Ohashi. Unlike her earlier years in elite gymnastics, where her life revolved almost entirely around training and competing the collegiate environment presented a different set of challenges. Juggling academics, social life, and the rigorous demands of gymnastics required her to adopt a more holistic approach, and in doing so, she discovered new ways to thrive inside and outside the gym.

Transitioning from the elite level of gymnastics, where training sessions could dominate the day, to the collegiate system came with its own unique set of pressures. At UCLA, Katelyn was no longer just a gymnast but a full-time student with academic responsibilities that demanded attention. This shift forced her to re-evaluate how she spent her time. Suddenly, managing schoolwork became as important as her training regimen. UCLA, a prestigious academic institution, set high expectations for its student-athletes, and Katelyn had to find a way to balance those with her athletic pursuits.

One of Katelyn's biggest adjustments was learning to manage her time efficiently. As an elite gymnast, her schedule had been dominated by training and competitions, often leaving little room for anything else. With the added coursework demands, she had to develop new habits and routines to ensure she could succeed academically and athletically. This often meant waking up early for classes, squeezing study sessions between training, and staying disciplined with deadlines. The ability to prioritize became essential as she navigated a world where success was not measured solely by performance on the mat but also by grades and academic achievements.

Gymnastics still played a significant role in her life, but the culture at UCLA allowed her to experience the sport differently. Instead of the cutthroat, high-pressure environment of elite gymnastics, collegiate gymnastics provided a more supportive and team-oriented atmosphere. This shift helped Katelyn better manage the pressure to perform at a high level while balancing her academic workload. The collegiate system offered a sense of camaraderie and community, where teammates shared the same struggles of balancing school, training, and personal life. This support network played a significant role in helping Katelyn manage the many demands placed on her.

While still intense, her gymnastics training had a different focus at the collegiate level. The emphasis was not solely on winning individual titles or pushing herself to extremes but on contributing to the team's success. This mindset shift allowed her to find more balance in her life. Practices were structured, and although they were still demanding, the environment encouraged her to enjoy the process more. This allowed Katelyn to develop a healthier relationship with the sport that had once been a source of immense pressure. Instead of being driven by the fear of failure or external expectations, she found motivation in her love for the sport and the joy of competing with her teammates.

Outside of gymnastics, Katelyn's college experience allowed her to explore interests beyond athletics. While her schedule remained packed, she engaged with other parts of campus life. This broader engagement had been largely absent during her elite gymnastics years, where the demands of the sport had left little room for other pursuits. At UCLA, she could meet new people, participate in student activities, and explore academic subjects that interested her. This new freedom, while still balanced with the responsibilities of gymnastics, helped Katelyn develop a more well-rounded identity.

A significant aspect of this balancing act was learning to care for herself mentally and physically. The rigorous training schedule and academic pressures could easily lead to burnout if not managed carefully. Katelyn became more attuned to her body's needs, understanding when to push and when to rest. Injuries taught her the importance of listening to her body, and now she applies those lessons in her daily life. Taking breaks, getting enough sleep, and managing stress were all part of the equation as she navigated the demands of being both a student and an athlete.

The mental toll of juggling so many responsibilities could not be ignored, and Katelyn had to find ways to cope with the stress of constantly shifting between different roles. UCLA provided resources for student-athletes, such as academic advisors and mental health support, which helped Katelyn maintain a sense of balance. She also leaned on her friends and teammates for emotional support, knowing they faced many of the same challenges. This sense of community and shared experience played a crucial role in keeping her grounded, particularly during times of high pressure, such as during finals or the lead-up to important competitions.

As Katelyn continued to develop outside of gymnastics, she found new passions that complemented her athletic career. She became increasingly interested in advocacy and using her platform to speak on issues that mattered to her, particularly around body positivity and mental health. This new sense of purpose gave her life outside of gymnastics even more meaning, and it was a reminder that her identity was not tied solely to her performance in the sport. Balancing these new interests with her gymnastics career and academics required careful time management, but it also gave her a sense of fulfillment that went beyond athletic success.

Another challenge Katelyn faced was balancing personal relationships amidst her busy schedule. Friendships and family time were often squeezed between practices, study sessions, and competitions, but Katelyn consciously maintained those connections. The support of her family, especially, had always been a cornerstone of her gymnastics journey, and keeping that connection strong was important to her. Additionally, building meaningful friendships with her teammates and classmates helped her navigate the complexities of college life. These relationships provided a sense of normalcy and grounded her, especially when the pressures of school and sports felt overwhelming.

One of Katelyn's most valuable lessons during this time was setting boundaries. With so many demands on her time and energy, it was easy to become overwhelmed. Setting clear boundaries, whether limiting social engagements during busy weeks or knowing when to ask for help with her coursework, became essential to maintaining balance. It wasn't always easy, but learning to say no when necessary allowed her to focus on the most important moment. Though challenging, this skill became a vital tool in her ability to succeed both in the classroom and the gym.

The experience of balancing school, gymnastics, and life outside the sport shaped Katelyn into a more resilient and adaptable person. She learned to manage her time effectively, prioritize her well-being, and embrace the challenges of juggling multiple roles. By the time she graduated from UCLA, Katelyn had achieved tremendous success in gymnastics and developed a strong sense of self that extended far beyond the gym. While not always easy, this balance allowed her to grow in ways she hadn't anticipated, and it became a defining aspect of her collegiate experience.

Chapter 5: The Perfect 10

Crafting the Iconic Floor Routine

Crafting an iconic floor routine is a unique blend of artistry, athleticism, and personal expression. For Katelyn Ohashi, this process became one of the defining aspects of her collegiate gymnastics career. When she arrived at UCLA, she was eager to embrace the opportunity to create a routine that showcased her technical skills and resonated with her personality and passions. This creative endeavor was far more than just a series of tumbling passes and dance elements; it was an opportunity for her to tell a story and connect with the audience in a way that left a lasting impact.

The journey toward developing her routine began with an exploration of her own identity. Katelyn understood that a successful floor routine must reflect who she was as a gymnast and person. This realization sparked a period of self-reflection that played a crucial role in shaping the themes and movements she wanted to incorporate. Katelyn found inspiration in various aspects of her life, from her cultural background to her love of music and dance. These influences guided her creative process, allowing her to craft an authentic and engaging performance.

Collaboration became a key element in creating her floor routine. Katelyn worked closely with her coach, Valorie Kondos Field, who encouraged her to embrace her individuality and explore her artistic side. This collaborative dynamic was instrumental in bringing Katelyn's vision to life. They brainstormed ideas and experimented with different choreography, combining athletic movements with expressive dance elements. This partnership fostered creativity and allowed Katelyn to feel supported in her artistic journey.

Music selection was another critical aspect of crafting Katelyn's routine. She wanted a piece that resonated with her and matched the energy she wished to convey. After much consideration, Katelyn chose to perform to a medley of popular songs, ultimately selecting "Get Your Freak On" by Missy Elliott. The upbeat tempo and infectious rhythm suited her vibrant personality and added an element of excitement to her performance. The choice of music set the tone for the routine and allowed her to incorporate movements that felt natural and expressive.

With the music in hand, Katelyn began translating her vision into choreography. The choreography needed to reflect her strengths as a gymnast and the story she wanted to tell. This meant that every movement had to serve a purpose, whether showcasing her powerful tumbling passes, elegant dance transitions, or expressive gestures. The routine became a fusion of her technical abilities and artistic flair, creating a dynamic performance that captivated audiences.

Rehearsing the routine was an essential part of the process. Katelyn dedicated countless hours to perfecting every element, ensuring that her movements flowed seamlessly from one to the next. This meticulous attention to detail was paramount in building her confidence. She practiced under the watchful eye of Coach Valorie, who provided constructive feedback and encouraged her to push the boundaries of her creativity. As the routine began to take shape, Katelyn discovered a new level of joy in her training. The creative process rekindled her passion for gymnastics, transforming her experience from one focused solely on competition to one that embraced the art of performance.

Incorporating dance elements was particularly important to Katelyn. She recognized that the floor routine was an opportunity to express herself through movement, and she wanted to showcase her love for dance and gymnastics. Katelyn included various dance styles in her routine, blending hip-hop, contemporary, and jazz influences. This fusion added a layer of complexity to her performance and allowed her to engage with the audience on a deeper level. Each movement was carefully crafted to enhance the narrative she aimed to convey, transforming her routine into a captivating visual experience.

As she continued to refine her choreography, Katelyn sought feedback not only from her coaches but also from her teammates. Their perspectives provided valuable insights and helped her see the routine differently. The collaborative spirit fostered a sense of camaraderie among the team, creating an environment where everyone felt empowered to express their creativity. This support network encouraged Katelyn to take risks and explore new ideas, ultimately leading to a more dynamic and engaging final product.

The routine's choreography was designed to highlight Katelyn's unique strengths. Her powerful tumbling passes showcased her athleticism, while the dance elements highlighted her grace and artistry. This duality became a hallmark of her performance, allowing her to connect with the audience on multiple levels. As Katelyn practiced, she discovered the power of storytelling through movement, understanding that each pass and pose contributed to the larger narrative she aimed to create.

The culmination of this creative process came during competitions. Katelyn approached each performance with a sense of excitement and anticipation. Stepping onto the mat was no longer just about executing skills; it was an opportunity to share her story with the world. Katelyn poured her heart and soul into every movement as she performed her routine. The combination of athleticism and artistry resonated with the audience, who responded with enthusiasm and energy.

Katelyn's routine not only earned high scores but also captured the attention of fans across the country. How she fused gymnastics with elements of dance and personal expression made her performances unforgettable. Each time she stepped onto the floor, she left a lasting impression, showcasing the beauty of gymnastics as a form of art. This newfound connection with the audience propelled her into the spotlight, turning her into a celebrated figure within the gymnastics community and beyond.

The iconic routine became more than just a series of movements; it was a testament to Katelyn's journey as an athlete and individual. She proved that gymnastics could be an avenue for self-expression, a platform to share one's identity with the world. As Katelyn continued to evolve as a gymnast, the creative process behind her floor routine remained a significant part of her story. It was a reminder of the joy she found in performance, the importance of collaboration, and the power of creativity to shape an athlete's journey.

Crafting this iconic routine became a defining moment in the grand scheme of her gymnastics career. It showcased her abilities as a gymnast and highlighted the beauty of vulnerability and authenticity. Katelyn Ohashi's floor routine was not just about winning medals or accolades; it celebrated individuality, creativity, and the transformative power of sport. She inspired countless young athletes through this creative process, encouraging them to embrace their uniqueness and express themselves fully in gymnastics and life.

The Moment of Perfection

On January 12, 2019, during a meet against the University of California, Berkeley, Katelyn Ohashi executed a floor routine that would resonate within the world of gymnastics and capture the hearts of millions around the globe. This performance was significant for many reasons, but what set it apart was its culmination in a perfect score of 10.0, a rarity in gymnastics that elicited overwhelming joy and excitement from everyone present. This moment transcended mere athletics; it became a celebration of artistry, individuality, and the beauty of sport.

As Katelyn prepared for her routine, she was excited and nervous. The atmosphere in the arena was electric, filled with fans who were there to support their teams and witness Katelyn's much-anticipated performance. Leading up to this moment, Katelyn had invested countless hours in practice, honing every element of her routine. She was keenly aware that this performance could be her opportunity to showcase her hard work and dedication on a national stage.

Stepping onto the floor, Katelyn felt the weight of anticipation. The arena erupted with applause as she took her position, a testament to the energy she had cultivated among her supporters. This was not just another routine; it was a chance to express herself and share her journey with those who had followed her path. The music started, and with it came a wave of adrenaline that surged through her. She began her routine with an explosive tumbling pass, landing firmly on her feet, and immediately, the audience erupted into cheers.

Katelyn's choreography blended powerful athleticism with fluid grace. Every movement was deliberate and infused with emotion, creating a captivating narrative that engaged spectators. The transitions from one skill to another flowed seamlessly, each element crafted to highlight her strengths and personality. She effortlessly combined complex tumbling passes with expressive dance, and each moment symbolized her identity as a gymnast. The routine was filled with elements that showcased her distinct style, including dramatic poses and energetic movements that resonated with the audience.

The highlight of her performance came during the final tumbling pass. Katelyn exuded confidence and control as she approached her last series of skills. Her final move, a stunning back handspring into a double tuck somersault, showcased her athletic prowess and artistry. The moment she landed, the crowd erupted into a frenzy, recognizing they had just witnessed something extraordinary. Katelyn stood tall, soaking in the applause, and the jubilant energy in the arena was palpable.

As the judges conferred, the excitement was thick with anticipation. The audience awaited the score, knowing that a perfect 10.0 would be a historic achievement, particularly in collegiate gymnastics, where such scores are seldom given. When the score flashed on the scoreboard, it felt like time stood still. A wave of disbelief and joy washed over Katelyn as the realization of her perfect score settled in. The number glowed brightly: 10.0. The arena erupted again, and Katelyn was met with roaring applause and cheers from her teammates, coaches, and the fans who had come to support her.

The viral nature of this moment was instant. Clips of her performance spread like wildfire on social media, capturing viewers' hearts far beyond the gymnastics community. People shared her routine, praising the technical excellence and the infectious joy and authenticity she brought to the performance. Commentators lauded her for reinventing the perception of gymnastics, merging athleticism with the joy of dance and personal expression. Katelyn's routine resonated with individuals of all ages, showcasing a unique blend of artistry that appealed to many beyond the traditional gymnastics audience.

For Katelyn, this achievement marked a significant turning point in her career. It validated her artistic approach to gymnastics and her decision to prioritize joy over the relentless pursuit of perfection often seen in the sport. The 10.0 score was not just a number; it represented a celebration of her journey, from her challenges as a young gymnast to her triumphs as a collegiate athlete. This moment became a powerful reminder of embracing one's uniqueness and sharing it with the world.

As the days turned into weeks following her viral performance, Katelyn was at the center of a media whirlwind. Interviews flooded in, and she symbolized positivity within the sport. She discussed her gymnastics philosophy, emphasizing that it should be about more than just competition. Katelyn expressed the importance of loving and finding happiness within the sport, inspiring many aspiring gymnasts to approach their training with a similar mindset. The perfect score elevated her status in gymnastics and made her a role model for countless young athletes striving to make their mark in the world of sport.

This moment of perfection also had a lasting impact on Katelyn's journey through collegiate gymnastics. Her performance encouraged her to continue exploring her artistic side, leading her to develop more innovative routines that reflected her individuality. The focus shifted from solely achieving high scores to embracing the joy of performance. Each time she stepped onto the mat, she carried the energy from that day, reminding herself that gymnastics could be a celebration of self-expression, creativity, and fun.

Katelyn Ohashi's moment of perfection resonated far beyond the gymnastics floor. It symbolized the power of artistry in athletics and the beauty of authenticity. Her ability to connect with the audience through her routine made a profound statement about what it means to be a gymnast. Her athleticism and artistry showcased a new narrative in gymnastics that values creativity, self-expression, and the joy of movement.

This historic performance was pivotal in Katelyn's life, opening doors to opportunities she had never imagined. The viral nature of her 10.0 routine brought her into the spotlight, allowing her to share her message of positivity and resilience with a wider audience. Katelyn's journey exemplifies the transformative power of sport, reminding us that the pursuit of excellence can be harmonized with the pursuit of joy.

The Media Frenzy and Global Recognition

After Katelyn Ohashi's electrifying floor routine earned a perfect 10.0 at the University of California meet, her life transformed overnight. The moment was not just a personal triumph; it became a global sensation that catapulted her into the media spotlight. The clip of her performance quickly went viral, amassing millions of views within days. Social media platforms erupted with praise and admiration, showcasing a blend of appreciation for her athletic prowess and the joy she brought to gymnastics. This sudden surge in recognition began a whirlwind of opportunities and challenges that Katelyn had to navigate.

The immediate aftermath of her performance was a flurry of activity. News outlets across the globe began to cover her story, celebrating her unique style and the infectious energy she exuded on the floor. Katelyn quickly became a household name, as her performance resonated with gymnastics enthusiasts and a wider audience who appreciated the emotional connection she forged during her routine. This unexpected fame brought a newfound platform, allowing her to influence discussions around the sport and advocate for a more inclusive and joyful approach to gymnastics.

As Katelyn adjusted to this sudden fame, the media frenzy intensified. Interviews poured in, and she navigated the complexities of public life. From television appearances to magazine features, Katelyn was thrust into the spotlight, where she spoke candidly about her experience and her views on gymnastics. The interview requests often came with tight deadlines and demanding schedules, but she handled them gracefully, understanding her voice's importance in promoting a positive message. She emphasized the significance of mental health and well-being in sports, which resonated with many young athletes and their families.

Amid this newfound attention, Katelyn remained grounded. She reflected on her journey, recognizing her struggles and the resilience it had instilled in her. The media often highlighted her previous challenges, including injuries and the pressure she had felt throughout her gymnastics career. These narratives became intertwined with her success, illustrating that her journey was not solely defined by her viral moment but rather by her perseverance in overcoming adversity. Katelyn's authenticity shone through as she shared her story, allowing fans and followers to connect with her on a deeper level.

As her profile grew, so did the demands of her schedule. Katelyn was invited to attend various events, from high-profile gymnastics competitions to award shows, where she was recognized for her contributions to the sport. Each appearance served as an opportunity to advocate for a shift in the gymnastics culture, one that prioritized joy and individuality over strict adherence to traditional expectations. She used these platforms to highlight the importance of mental health, encouraging young athletes to prioritize their well-being alongside their athletic pursuits.

Global recognition has also opened doors to exciting partnerships and endorsements. Brands began to reach out to Katelyn, eager to collaborate with someone who embodied the spirit of empowerment and positivity. Her influence extended beyond gymnastics, resonating with individuals from all walks of life inspired by her journey. Katelyn became an ambassador for various causes, leveraging her platform to bring awareness to issues close to her heart. Whether it was promoting body positivity or encouraging young girls to embrace their unique identities, she embraced the role of a role model wholeheartedly.

Despite the whirlwind of fame, Katelyn remained focused on her gymnastics career. She understood that while the media attention was exhilarating, it was crucial to maintain her passion for the sport. Balancing training with her newfound obligations required careful planning and support from her team. Katelyn worked closely with her coaches to ensure that she continued to develop her skills while managing her schedule effectively. They established a routine that allowed her to prioritize her training and commitments, ensuring she stayed connected to the sport she loved.

The viral success of her routine also sparked a broader conversation about the culture of gymnastics. Fans and commentators began to reflect on the often high-pressure environment gymnasts faced, and

Katelyn's message of joy resonated widely. She became a voice for change within the gymnastics community, advocating for a shift from perfectionism to celebrating individuality and creativity. Her approach encouraged coaches, parents, and athletes to rethink their perspectives on success and to prioritize the joy of movement over the pursuit of flawless performances.

As Katelyn navigated her new reality, she often reflected on the impact of her sudden fame. While the recognition brought exciting opportunities, it also came with its own set of challenges. The constant scrutiny of her performances and public appearances could sometimes be overwhelming. However, she remained resilient, reminding herself of the reasons she had fallen in love with gymnastics in the first place. This foundation kept her grounded, allowing her to focus on what truly mattered: her passion for the sport and the joy it brought her.

The journey following her viral moment highlighted the importance of mental health in athletics. Katelyn advocated for self-care, emphasizing that success should not come at the cost of one's well-being. She encouraged fellow gymnasts to listen to their bodies, recognize their limits, and seek help. By sharing her experiences and promoting an open dialogue around mental health, Katelyn aimed to create a supportive environment for athletes at all levels.

As Katelyn embraced her public figure role, she remained committed to her training. The duality of being both an athlete and a media personality required her to adapt quickly and prioritize her goals. She understood that maintaining her competitive edge was essential to her identity as a gymnast, and she worked tirelessly to balance her responsibilities. Katelyn's dedication to her craft and ability to share her journey with others set her apart as a unique figure in gymnastics.

Through it all, Katelyn Ohashi remained true to herself. The overnight fame and media frenzy did not define her; instead, they provided her a platform to inspire others and advocate for change.

Her journey serves as a reminder that success can be redefined and that joy and authenticity coexist with high-level competition. The legacy of her viral moment continues to influence young gymnasts, encouraging them to embrace their individuality and approach the sport with a sense of passion and purpose.

In reflecting on her path, Katelyn recognized the significance of her impact. The media attention may have brought challenges, but it also allowed her to advocate for a more positive culture in gymnastics. By sharing her story and championing a joyful approach to the sport, Katelyn has inspired countless individuals to pursue their passions unapologetically. Her journey reminds us all that true success lies not in perfection but in the courage to be ourselves.

Chapter 6: Battling Body Image and Mental Health Challenges

Behind the Scenes

Spectacular performances and a personal struggle with body image and self-worth marked Katelyn Ohashi's journey through gymnastics. Behind the scenes of her success lay a complex narrative shaped by the relentless scrutiny that comes with competing at the highest level. The sport's culture often emphasizes a specific body type, fostering an environment where athletes feel inadequate regardless of their skills and achievements. This reality was particularly challenging for Katelyn as she grappled with the expectations imposed by coaches, judges, and even social media.

From a young age, Katelyn exhibited immense talent and dedication. However, as she rose through the ranks, she became increasingly aware of the societal pressures surrounding athletes, especially female gymnasts. The idealization of a particular physique, thin, toned, and almost weightless, created a dichotomy between her body and the image she felt was expected of her. This conflict intensified as she transitioned into elite gymnastics, where judges often emphasized appearance alongside performance. The cumulative impact of these factors took a toll on her mental health as she began to internalize feelings of inadequacy and self-doubt.

Social media further complicated Katelyn's relationship with her body. The platforms that could serve as a source of connection and support also became spaces for comparison and judgment. As she navigated her rise to fame, she was subjected to comments that critiqued her appearance, undermining her confidence and exacerbating her struggles with body image. The noise of public opinion often drowned out her accomplishments, leading her to question her worth as an athlete and individual. Despite her successes, the constant scrutiny fostered a sense of insecurity that lingered beneath the surface.

In grappling with these issues, Katelyn sought solace in training and cultivating relationships within the gymnastics community. Her coaches, teammates, and family played pivotal roles in supporting her through this tumultuous period. They encouraged her to focus on her strengths and the joy of gymnastics rather than the pressures of external expectations. This network provided a safe space for Katelyn to express her feelings, helping her confront her challenges head-on. However, even with this support, the journey to self-acceptance was not straightforward. Katelyn often found herself torn between the desire to conform to the expectations of the sport and the need to embrace her individuality.

As she navigated these turbulent waters, Katelyn discovered the power of vulnerability. Opening up about her struggles became a transformative experience. By sharing her story, she realized that many athletes faced similar challenges and that their shared experiences could foster community and understanding. Katelyn recognized the importance of speaking out against body shaming for herself and others who were grappling with their self-worth. By shedding light on her journey, she hoped to challenge the harmful narratives that permeated the sport and promote a more inclusive perspective on being a successful gymnast.

Through this process, Katelyn developed a newfound appreciation for her body as a vessel for strength and expression. She started to celebrate her unique qualities, understanding that her value extended far beyond her physical appearance. The routines she performed became a reflection of her passion and creativity rather than a means to fit into a narrow definition of beauty. This shift in mindset allowed her to reconnect with the joy of gymnastics, liberating her from the confines of societal expectations.

The emotional journey was marked by moments of doubt and triumph. As Katelyn worked to rebuild her self-esteem, she faced setbacks that tested her resolve. In times of struggle, she often turned to her coaches and teammates for guidance, finding comfort in their unwavering support. This network served as a reminder that success in gymnastics is not solely measured by scores or accolades but also by the connections forged through shared experiences and the strength to overcome adversity.

Katelyn's candid discussions about body image resonated with many fans, especially young athletes who looked up to her. She became a beacon of hope for those feeling marginalized by the prevailing beauty standards in sports. Her willingness to address the struggles of body shaming prompted conversations that extended beyond gymnastics, highlighting the importance of mental health and self-acceptance in all areas of life. The conversations surrounding body positivity began to permeate the gymnastics community, inspiring a shift in how athletes viewed their bodies and worth.

As Katelyn continued to grow, she made it a priority to advocate for change within gymnastics. She collaborated with organizations that promoted body positivity and mental well-being, striving to create a more supportive environment for young gymnasts. Her efforts were aimed at challenging the status quo, encouraging athletes to embrace their individuality and redefine what it means to be successful. Katelyn's voice became a powerful tool for change, helping to dismantle the stigma surrounding body image and paving the way for future generations of athletes.

In time, Katelyn's journey of self-acceptance culminated in a deeper understanding of her identity as an athlete. She realized that her body was not just a means to execute perfect routines but a source of strength and resilience. Her struggles made her more compassionate and empathetic, allowing her to connect with others profoundly. This newfound perspective helped her to navigate the complexities of competitive gymnastics while remaining true to herself.

The legacy Katelyn built extended beyond her achievements in the gym. By championing the importance of mental health and self-acceptance, she inspired a movement that resonated with many athletes across various disciplines. Her story became a testament to the power of vulnerability, demonstrating that it is possible to thrive even amidst adversity. Katelyn's influence encouraged athletes to embrace their authentic selves, creating a ripple effect that fostered a culture of acceptance and support.

Reflecting on her journey, Katelyn Ohashi became a powerful advocate for change in gymnastics and beyond. Her challenges with body image and self-worth ultimately fueled her passion for promoting a more inclusive and positive environment. She has empowered countless individuals to embrace their uniqueness and prioritize their mental well-being through her advocacy. Katelyn's story serves as a reminder that the true measure of success lies not in conforming to societal expectations but in the courage to celebrate one's authentic self. The struggles she encountered on her path have shaped her into a role model for future generations, inspiring them to pursue their passions with confidence and pride.

Breaking the Silence

Katelyn Ohashi's journey through gymnastics was defined by her athletic prowess and commitment to challenging the sport's unrealistic beauty standards. As she rose to fame, she became increasingly aware of the societal pressures that affected her and countless young athletes who looked up to her. Katelyn's story is one of resilience and courage, as she took a stand against the relentless scrutiny of bodies in gymnastics, advocating for a more inclusive and supportive environment.

From a young age, Katelyn was immersed in a world that idolized a specific physique, a world that often equated athletic success with conforming to narrow beauty ideals. As she transitioned to elite gymnastics, the pressure intensified. It became evident that being recognized for her talent was often overshadowed by judgments related to her appearance. This duality weighed heavily on her, creating an internal conflict many athletes can relate to. Katelyn's experience reflected a broader issue within competitive sports, where emphasis on appearance can overshadow an athlete's capabilities and achievements.

Katelyn's rise to prominence began with her exceptional skills on the mat, yet she soon grappled with the pressure to fit a mold that did not represent her true self. Competing at high-profile events, she encountered a culture prioritizing specific body types, often ignoring the strength and athleticism defining a gymnast. This external pressure made her question her worth beyond the performances, fostering insecurities that would haunt her for years. The challenges she faced were not merely personal; they echoed a collective struggle among female athletes who felt compelled to meet unrealistic standards.

The turning point for Katelyn came during introspection, where she began to realize the importance of authenticity and self-acceptance. Armed with this newfound perspective, she decided to use her platform to address the harmful narratives surrounding beauty in gymnastics. This marked the beginning of her courageous stand against the unrealistic expectations that had plagued her and many others. Katelyn began speaking openly about her battles with body image, encouraging others to embrace their unique forms and celebrate their journeys.

As she publicly shared her experiences, Katelyn became a voice for those who felt silenced by the relentless expectations imposed upon them. Her willingness to confront these issues head-on resonated with many, especially young gymnasts who often felt pressured to conform to a certain aesthetic. By shining a light on the negative impact of body shaming, Katelyn sparked important conversations about self-worth, mental health, and the need for systemic change within the sport.

Katelyn's commitment to breaking the silence surrounding beauty standards extended beyond social media. She began engaging with gymnastics organizations and advocacy groups, pushing for reforms to create a more supportive environment for athletes of all shapes and sizes. Her efforts aimed to foster a culture where performance, dedication, and passion for the sport precede appearance. Katelyn sought to dismantle the toxic narrative that had long pervaded gymnastics and encourage a more compassionate approach to athlete development by championing inclusivity.

The response to Katelyn's advocacy was overwhelmingly positive, as many recognized the necessity for change within the gymnastics community. Young athletes began to speak out about their own experiences, sharing stories of feeling marginalized or judged based on their bodies. Katelyn's bravery empowered them to challenge the status quo, reinforcing that true beauty lies in diversity and strength rather than conformity. The ripple effect of her actions contributed to a growing movement advocating for body positivity and mental health awareness in sports.

Through her platform, Katelyn highlighted the importance of mental health, recognizing that the pressures associated with elite gymnastics could lead to detrimental effects on an athlete's well-being. By encouraging conversations around mental health, she aimed to destigmatize these issues, allowing athletes to seek help without fear of judgment. Katelyn's advocacy served as a reminder that athletes are not just competitors but individuals with their struggles, dreams, and aspirations.

As Katelyn continued her fight against unrealistic beauty standards, she became influential in the push for reform within gymnastics. Her work sparked a broader dialogue about prioritizing health and wellness over appearance. Gymnastics organizations began to take notice, initiating discussions about policies that would create a more inclusive and supportive environment for athletes. Katelyn's courageous stand was crucial in challenging outdated norms and fostering a culture that values athletes for their skills and contributions rather than their looks.

The journey was not without its challenges. Katelyn faced backlash from some corners of the gymnastics community, where traditional views regarding beauty and performance were deeply entrenched. However, she remained steadfast in her mission, understanding that progress often comes with resistance. Katelyn's resolve only strengthened her commitment to advocating for change as she continued to share her message with unwavering determination.

Over time, Katelyn's influence transcended gymnastics. Her story resonated with individuals across various disciplines, igniting a broader conversation about body image and self-acceptance in sports and beyond. She became a symbol of empowerment, inspiring people to challenge the societal norms that dictate how we perceive beauty. Katelyn's legacy is not just defined by her achievements in the gym but by her role as a catalyst for change, reminding athletes everywhere that their worth is inherent and not dictated by their appearance.

In competitive sports, Katelyn Ohashi's courageous stand against unrealistic beauty standards represents a significant shift toward inclusivity and acceptance. Her advocacy resonates with countless individuals, fostering a movement prioritizing mental health, self-love, and authenticity. Katelyn's journey reminds us all that embracing our unique selves and challenging the norms that seek to define us is acceptable and essential. Through her work, she has paved the way for future generations of athletes, ensuring that they can pursue their passions without the burden of unrealistic expectations. Katelyn's voice remains a powerful reminder that true strength lies in physical ability and the courage to stand up for oneself and others.

Embracing Body Positivity

Katelyn Ohashi's journey toward embracing body positivity is a remarkable tale of personal transformation and empowerment. For many years, the pressures of competitive gymnastics led her to struggle with self-acceptance. As a young athlete, Katelyn was inundated with messages prioritizing appearance over performance. The constant scrutiny from judges, coaches, and media created an environment where her worth was often measured by her physical form rather than her immense talent and dedication to the sport. However, her evolution into a body positivity advocate showcases the resilience of the human spirit and the power of self-love.

In her earlier years, Katelyn was caught in the grip of perfectionism, a common trait among elite athletes. She was aware of the expectations surrounding her, not just as a gymnast but as a public figure. The emphasis on being slender and fit often overshadowed her achievements, leading her to internalize the belief that her body needed to conform to a specific standard. This mindset manifested in various ways, including unhealthy dieting and excessive workouts, all in pursuit of an ideal that felt increasingly unattainable. Each competition was not merely a test of skill but a reminder of her appearance, resulting in a toxic relationship with her body that overshadowed her love for gymnastics.

The turning point came during a critical moment in her career when she began to reassess her relationship with her body and self-worth. Katelyn realized that her identity could not be confined to the narrow expectations the sport or society placed upon her. This shift in perspective marked the beginning of her journey toward self-acceptance. She began to embrace her body for what it was: strong, capable, and uniquely hers. This realization did not happen overnight; rather, it was a gradual process of redefining her self-image and recognizing her value beyond physical appearance.

Katelyn's journey towards body positivity was also influenced by the support of friends, family, and mentors who encouraged her to celebrate her individuality. They emphasized that her value lay in her abilities and character rather than the number on a scale. Their encouragement provided Katelyn with a solid foundation upon which she could build her newfound self-esteem. As she began to share her story, she discovered that many young athletes faced similar struggles, trapped in a cycle of comparison and self-doubt. Recognizing this commonality became a powerful motivator for her to advocate for body positivity.

Katelyn started sharing candid posts about her experiences through her social media platforms, highlighting her triumphs and challenges. She openly discussed her struggles with body image, revealing the pressures she felt and how they impacted her mental health. This vulnerability resonated with many, as it provided a relatable narrative in a world that often promotes unattainable ideals. Katelyn's authenticity became a breath of fresh air in a landscape saturated with curated perfection, encouraging others to embrace their flaws and celebrate their uniqueness.

Katelyn also became involved in various body positivity initiatives, collaborating with organizations that promote self-acceptance and mental health awareness. She began participating in workshops and speaking engagements, where she could share her journey and empower others to cultivate a positive body image. Through these efforts, she aimed to shift the narrative surrounding athleticism and beauty, emphasizing that all bodies deserve respect and admiration. Her message was clear: self-love and acceptance are vital to overall well-being.

As Katelyn's platform grew, so did her impact. She began to notice changes within the gymnastics community, where discussions about body image and mental health took center stage. Coaches and organizations began to recognize the importance of fostering an environment that promotes self-acceptance rather than conformity to unrealistic standards. Katelyn's advocacy opened doors for young gymnasts to express themselves freely, allowing them to focus on their skills without the weight of societal expectations.

Through her journey, Katelyn learned that embracing body positivity is not a linear path; it involves ongoing self-reflection and growth. There were moments of vulnerability and doubt, but each time she faced these challenges, she emerged stronger and more resilient. She discovered that true confidence comes from within, stemming from a deep understanding and appreciation of oneself. This self-awareness became a cornerstone of her advocacy, encouraging others to embark on their journeys of self-discovery.

In sharing her story, Katelyn hoped to inspire a generation of young athletes to redefine what it means to be successful. She emphasized that success is not solely measured by medals or accolades but by the ability to love oneself and pursue one's passions without external pressures. Her message resonated widely, touching the hearts of individuals from all walks of life who had faced similar battles with self-worth and acceptance.

Katelyn's commitment to body positivity also influenced her approach to training. As she embraced her body, she learned to listen to its needs, understanding that health encompasses more than just physical appearance. This holistic perspective led to a more balanced approach to her training, prioritizing mental and emotional well-being alongside physical strength. She began to appreciate the incredible capabilities of her body, celebrating its resilience and power rather than fixating on how it looked.

The journey toward self-acceptance ultimately became a source of empowerment for Katelyn and countless others who followed her story. As she continued to advocate for body positivity, she inspired individuals to embrace their authentic selves and redefine their relationship with their bodies. Katelyn Ohashi's transformation is a testament to the importance of self-love, resilience, and the courage to challenge societal norms.

Katelyn has created a ripple effect through her advocacy, encouraging discussions about body image and mental health in sports and beyond. Her influence extends far beyond the gymnastics mat, as she inspires individuals to challenge the societal expectations that seek to define their worth. By championing body positivity, Katelyn has become a beacon of hope for those who struggle with self-acceptance, empowering them to embrace their unique journeys and recognize that their value transcends appearance.

As she continues to advocate for change, Katelyn Ohashi exemplifies the transformative power of embracing body positivity. Her journey encourages all individuals to recognize their worth, celebrate their individuality, and cultivate a loving relationship with themselves. In a world that often promotes unrealistic beauty standards, Katelyn's message stands out as a powerful reminder that true beauty lies in authenticity, strength, and the courage to be oneself. Through her ongoing efforts, Katelyn is shaping a more inclusive future for athletes everywhere, fostering a culture where self-acceptance reigns supreme.

Chapter 7: Becoming an Advocate

Speaking Out on Mental Health

Katelyn Ohashi's commitment to advocating mental health awareness has evolved significantly throughout her career. As a gymnast who has experienced the intense pressures of competition firsthand, she has recognized the vital importance of mental well-being for herself and all athletes. With the increasing focus on performance and perfection in sports, many young athletes face unprecedented challenges that can impact their mental health. Katelyn's experiences and openness about her struggles have positioned her as a leading voice in the movement to raise awareness about mental health in athletics.

From a young age, Katelyn was aware of the toll that gymnastics could take on one's mental health. The sport demands not only physical strength but also mental fortitude. The relentless pursuit of perfection can lead to feelings of anxiety, stress, and even depression. Throughout her career, Katelyn grappled with these pressures, often feeling that her worth was tied to her performance. This connection between performance and self-worth is a common struggle for many athletes, especially those competing at elite levels. As Katelyn transitioned through various phases of her gymnastics journey, she learned to confront these challenges and seek help when needed.

Katelyn's path toward understanding the importance of mental health took shape during her formative years in gymnastics. Like many athletes, she had been conditioned to prioritize physical strength and skills above all else. However, after enduring injuries and the emotional fallout from them, she began to recognize that mental resilience was just as crucial as physical training. These experiences prompted her to re-evaluate her approach to gymnastics and overall well-being. It became clear to her that a healthy mind is essential for achieving peak performance and enjoying the sport she loved.

In her efforts to speak out about mental health, Katelyn has made it a priority to share her personal experiences openly. She recognizes that many young athletes struggle in silence, often feeling alone in their battles with mental health issues. By sharing her story, Katelyn aims to create a sense of community and understanding among athletes, encouraging them to seek help and support. Her willingness to be vulnerable has resonated with many, as it sheds light on athletes' often-overlooked emotional challenges.

Through social media platforms and public speaking engagements, Katelyn has advocated for normalizing conversations surrounding mental health in sports. She has emphasized that discussing mental health should not be stigmatized or viewed as a weakness. Instead, it should be recognized as an essential aspect of overall well-being for every athlete's success. Katelyn's message is clear: prioritizing mental health is acceptable and necessary for athletes to perform at their best.

Katelyn's advocacy extends beyond her own experiences; she has actively participated in campaigns and initiatives to promote mental health awareness among athletes. She has collaborated with organizations that focus on mental health resources for young athletes, providing them with tools and support to navigate the pressures of their sport. By working with these organizations, Katelyn aims to ensure that athletes can access mental health resources and understand the importance of seeking help.

One significant aspect of Katelyn's advocacy is her emphasis on the need for open dialogues within sports communities. She believes that coaches, parents, and fellow athletes should foster an environment where discussing mental health is encouraged and normalized. Creating a culture of openness can help reduce the stigma surrounding mental health struggles, allowing athletes to feel comfortable sharing their feelings and seeking assistance. Katelyn has often highlighted the role that coaches play in this process, urging them to be attentive to the mental well-being of their athletes and to prioritize mental health as part of training.

Katelyn's influence has sparked broader discussions about mental health within the gymnastics community and beyond. Her raised awareness has inspired athletes and organizations to consider mental health a fundamental aspect of training and competition. Many gymnastics programs have begun integrating mental health resources into their training regimens, recognizing the importance of nurturing the mind and body. This shift represents a significant step forward in recognizing mental health in sports, illustrating how Katelyn's advocacy is making a tangible impact.

As Katelyn continues her advocacy work, she remains committed to educating athletes about the signs of mental health issues and the importance of self-care. She encourages them to recognize the signs of burnout, anxiety, and depression and urges them to prioritize their mental well-being alongside their physical training. Through workshops and seminars, Katelyn has reached a wide audience, offering insights into cultivating mental resilience and coping with the pressures of competitive sports.

Katelyn's message is particularly important for younger athletes, who are often more vulnerable to mental health challenges due to societal pressures and expectations. By sharing her story and providing guidance, she aims to empower the next generation of athletes to prioritize their mental health and embrace their individuality. Katelyn believes fostering a positive mindset is essential for success, and she encourages young athletes to define their worth beyond the realm of sports.

Her dedication to mental health advocacy has also sparked conversations about the role of parents in supporting their children's mental well-being. Katelyn emphasizes that parents should encourage open discussions about feelings and mental health, allowing their children to express themselves without fear of judgment. By promoting understanding and support, parents can play a crucial role in their children's mental health journey, helping them confidently navigate the challenges of competitive sports.

As Katelyn continues raising awareness about mental health among athletes, she remains dedicated to self-care and personal growth. She recognizes that mental health is an ongoing journey that requires constant attention and effort. By prioritizing her mental well-being, Katelyn exemplifies the importance of self-care, demonstrating to others that it is essential to nourish both the body and mind.

Katelyn Ohashi's advocacy for mental health awareness has become a powerful force in the sports community. Through her openness, dedication, and determination, she has inspired countless athletes to prioritize their mental well-being and seek help. By challenging mental health stigma, Katelyn has created a space where athletes can feel empowered to share their experiences and advocate for themselves and others. Her work represents a significant shift in how mental health is perceived in athletics, fostering a culture where well-being is recognized as essential to success. As she continues to speak out and support fellow athletes, Katelyn's impact will undoubtedly resonate for years, paving the way for a healthier, more understanding future in sports.

Advocating for Body Positivity

Katelyn Ohashi's advocacy for body positivity has become a powerful component of her identity as an athlete and public figure. Throughout her career, she has faced the pressures and expectations imposed by society and the gymnastics community regarding body image. Her journey toward self-acceptance and confidence has inspired many, and she has utilized her platform to encourage others to embrace their bodies and reject unrealistic beauty standards.

Katelyn's story began in the competitive world of gymnastics, where the emphasis on aesthetics and body shape is particularly pronounced. She knew body image was intertwined with athletic performance from an early age. Gymnasts are often scrutinized for their skills and appearance, which can create immense pressure to conform to a narrow ideal. This pressure weighed heavily on Katelyn as she navigated her gymnastics career, leading her to struggle with her self-image.

As Katelyn gained recognition for her talent, she became a target for praise and criticism. The scrutiny she faced became a double-edged sword; while her achievements were celebrated, the public also dissected her body. Such comments led her to internalize that her worth was tied to how she looked, contributing to the challenges she faced with body image. This environment fostered a sense of disconnection from her own body, creating a conflict between her love for gymnastics and the external pressures to maintain a certain appearance.

Realizing the detrimental impact of these societal standards, Katelyn embarked on a journey to redefine her relationship with her body. She began challenging the conventional notions of beauty that had influenced her for so long. Through her experiences, she discovered the importance of self-love and acceptance. This transformative journey allowed her to embrace her unique qualities, ultimately contributing to her personal and athletic growth. Katelyn recognized that body positivity is not just about physical appearance but about honoring oneself, regardless of how closely one aligns with societal ideals.

In her quest for self-acceptance, Katelyn found strength in vulnerability. She began to share her story with audiences, using her platform to raise awareness about the harmful effects of body shaming and the unrealistic expectations that permeate the world of sports. She expressed her commitment to promoting body positivity and encouraging others to embrace individuality through interviews, social media, and public speaking engagements. By sharing her struggles, Katelyn opened the door for conversations that had often been silenced, empowering others to speak out about their own experiences.

Katelyn's message resonated deeply with many, particularly young athletes grappling with body image issues. By highlighting her journey, she provided a relatable narrative that many found comfort in. She emphasized that it is okay to have insecurities and that these feelings are shared by countless individuals, regardless of their success or public persona. Katelyn's willingness to be honest about her challenges fostered a sense of connection and solidarity among her followers, creating a supportive community focused on acceptance.

Advocating for body positivity also meant Katelyn had to confront her internalized beliefs. She worked diligently to shift her mindset and embrace a healthier perspective on her body. Through self-reflection and positive affirmations, she learned to appreciate her body for its capabilities rather than its appearance. This shift was instrumental in her journey, allowing her to reclaim her sense of self and enjoy gymnastics without the burden of external expectations.

Katelyn's advocacy extended beyond personal narratives; she actively participated in campaigns promoting body positivity in sports. Collaborating with organizations dedicated to mental health and self-acceptance, she leveraged her influence to reach broader audiences. Katelyn's involvement in these initiatives highlighted the importance of creating environments where athletes can thrive without the weight of body image issues. Her commitment to these causes underscored that self-acceptance is crucial for individual athletes and the entire sports community.

Through her powerful platform, Katelyn also addressed the need for systemic change within gymnastics and other sports. She called for a cultural shift that prioritizes mental health and body positivity alongside athletic performance. Katelyn emphasized that organizations must take responsibility for creating supportive environments that celebrate diversity and encourage athletes to appreciate their bodies for their unique qualities. By advocating for policy changes, she aimed to influence the next generation of athletes, ensuring they feel empowered to embrace their individuality rather than conform to unrealistic standards.

Katelyn's commitment to body positivity reached a global audience, inspiring countless individuals to reassess their perceptions of beauty. Her story has sparked conversations about representation and inclusivity, emphasizing the need for diverse bodies to be celebrated in sports and media. Katelyn's visibility as a body positivity advocate has been pivotal in challenging the traditional narratives surrounding athleticism and appearance. By normalizing conversations about body image, she has encouraged others to advocate for themselves and strive for a more inclusive understanding of beauty.

In her pursuit of body positivity, Katelyn has also highlighted the significance of self-care. She has often spoken about prioritizing mental and emotional well-being, recognizing that body image is intrinsically linked to overall health. Katelyn has inspired others to cultivate a positive relationship with their bodies by promoting practices that foster self-love and acceptance. She encourages individuals to focus on their strengths, passions, and achievements, reinforcing that true beauty comes from within.

Katelyn Ohashi's journey of advocating for body positivity is a testament to the power of self-acceptance and the importance of challenging societal norms. Her courageous stand against unrealistic beauty standards inspired many to embrace their bodies and celebrate their individuality. Katelyn's influence has sparked conversations about body image and mental health, encouraging athletes and individuals to prioritize their well-being. As she continues to share her story on global platforms, Katelyn remains a beacon of hope and empowerment for those striving to find their place in a world that often imposes rigid beauty standards. Her advocacy reflects a growing movement toward inclusivity and acceptance, fostering a culture where all bodies are celebrated for their uniqueness and strength.

Inspiring the Next Generation

Katelyn Ohashi's journey in gymnastics has transformed her into a powerful role model for young athletes. Her experiences, struggles, and triumphs resonate deeply with aspiring gymnasts and those in sports, providing them invaluable lessons beyond the gym. Through her candid storytelling and unwavering dedication to body positivity and mental health, Katelyn aims to inspire the next generation to pursue their passions with confidence, resilience, and authenticity.

From her early days in gymnastics, Katelyn faced the intense pressure of being an elite athlete. The demands of training, competition, and performance can be overwhelming for anyone, but she navigated these challenges in the public eye. Rather than allowing the weight of expectations to deter her, Katelyn learned to embrace her individuality and the unique qualities that set her apart. This realization has been central to her message for young athletes: to be true to themselves, regardless of their external pressures.

Katelyn often emphasizes the importance of self-acceptance and healthy relationships with one's body. Many young athletes look up to her for her athletic accomplishments and her courageous stance against unrealistic beauty standards. By openly discussing her struggles with body image, she has provided a voice for those who feel isolated in their experiences. She encourages young gymnasts to prioritize self-love and to understand that their worth is not dictated by their appearance but by their hard work, dedication, and passion for the sport.

As an advocate for mental health, Katelyn urges young athletes to recognize the significance of their emotional well-being. She shares her journey of overcoming challenges related to performance anxiety and self-doubt, illustrating that these feelings are common and can be addressed. Her honesty about the mental toll of elite sports resonates with many young athletes grappling with similar issues. Katelyn's message is clear: seeking help is not a sign of weakness but an essential part of maintaining a healthy mindset in the competitive world of sports.

Katelyn frequently reminds young athletes to focus on their journeys rather than comparing themselves to others. The gymnastics community can sometimes foster an environment where comparisons are rampant, leading to feelings of inadequacy. Katelyn's experiences have taught her that every athlete has a unique path and that progress is not always linear. She encourages young gymnasts to celebrate their milestones, regardless of how they measure up against their peers. This perspective allows athletes to foster a sense of accomplishment and joy in their training rather than succumbing to the pressure of perfectionism.

Another key aspect of Katelyn's message to young athletes is the importance of passion and joy in sports. While pursuing excellence is a common goal among athletes, Katelyn emphasizes that the love for the sport should remain at the forefront. She encourages young gymnasts to remember why they began their journey in the first place, often recalling the sheer joy of flipping, twisting, and soaring through the air. By nurturing this passion, athletes can create a fulfilling and sustainable relationship with their sport, making it a source of happiness rather than solely a path to success.

Katelyn also advocates that athletes should feel empowered to speak out about their experiences. She believes sharing stories fosters connection and helps break down barriers within the athletic community. By encouraging young athletes to voice their thoughts, feelings, and concerns, Katelyn promotes an atmosphere of support and understanding. This approach helps individuals feel less alone in their struggles. It cultivates a culture where athletes can advocate for their needs, whether it pertains to mental health, training environments, or body positivity.

In her interactions with young athletes, Katelyn emphasizes the importance of resilience and perseverance. The road to success in gymnastics is often riddled with setbacks, injuries, and disappointments. Rather than allowing these challenges to define them, Katelyn encourages athletes to view obstacles as opportunities for growth. She shares her own experiences of bouncing back from injuries and setbacks, demonstrating that resilience is a skill that can be cultivated. Young athletes learn that the ability to adapt, learn, and continue striving toward their goals is what truly sets successful individuals apart.

As Katelyn travels to schools, gymnastics clubs, and various events, her influence extends beyond her achievements. She is a beacon of hope and empowerment for aspiring athletes from all backgrounds. By advocating for inclusivity in sports, she stresses that everyone deserves a place in gymnastics, regardless of their body type, skill level, or background. Katelyn's emphasis on diversity fosters an environment where young athletes can see themselves represented in the sport, inspiring them to chase their dreams confidently.

In addition to her advocacy work, Katelyn has harnessed the power of social media to connect with young athletes globally. She shares motivational messages, workout tips, and personal reflections that resonate with her audience through her platforms. Katelyn's engaging content encourages athletes to interact, ask questions, and share their stories. This sense of community is vital for young athletes who may feel isolated in their journey, as they find support and encouragement from fellow athletes who understand their struggles and aspirations.

Katelyn's commitment to inspiring the next generation of athletes extends to her belief in the power of mentorship. She frequently speaks about the importance of role models in shaping the journeys of young athletes. By encouraging experienced athletes to share their knowledge and experiences, Katelyn advocates for a culture of mentorship within the gymnastics community. She believes that mentorship enhances skill development and nurtures emotional growth, helping young athletes navigate the complexities of competitive sports.

Katelyn Ohashi's impact on young athletes transcends gymnastics; her message resonates with individuals across various sports and disciplines. Through her journey of self-acceptance, mental health advocacy, and commitment to body positivity, she inspires aspiring athletes to embrace their unique paths and pursue their passions with confidence. Katelyn's emphasis on joy, resilience, and community cultivates a new generation of athletes equipped to face challenges head-on while remaining true to themselves. As she continues to share her story and engage with young athletes, Katelyn Ohashi remains a symbol of hope, empowerment, and authenticity in the world of sports.

Chapter 8: Life Beyond the Mat

Retirement from Gymnastics

As Katelyn Ohashi approached the decision to retire from gymnastics, a complex tapestry of emotions intertwined, merging excitement for new beginnings with a profound sense of loss. For years, gymnastics had been the focal point of her life, a rigorous pursuit that shaped her identity and provided a platform for self-expression. However, as she reflected on her journey, it became clear that stepping away from the sport was necessary for her evolution, allowing her to explore new avenues and embrace a different chapter in her life.

Retirement from gymnastics is rarely straightforward, especially for an athlete like Katelyn, who had dedicated herself to the sport with unwavering passion. The rigorous training, the exhilarating performances, and the relationships formed along the way all contributed to her growth as an athlete and a person. Yet, after years of competing at an elite level, Katelyn began to feel the weight of her decision to step away from the sport that had been her entire world.

The physical toll of gymnastics is significant, and Katelyn's body had endured countless hours of training, injuries, and the demands of high-level competition. As she contemplated her future, she understood that her body was sending signals that it needed a break. The desire to maintain her physical health and well-being grew stronger, nudging her to realize that her time in gymnastics was reaching its natural conclusion. The challenge was reconciling this need with her emotional connection to the sport that had defined her life for so long.

Katelyn also grappled with the psychological aspects of retirement. Athletes often experience a sense of identity crisis when stepping away from their sport. For years, she had been known as a gymnast, recognized for her incredible talent and remarkable performances. The thought of no longer being identified by her athletic accomplishments stirred feelings of uncertainty. Who would she be outside of gymnastics? How would she navigate a world where her identity was no longer tied to her routines, medals, and competitions? These questions lingered in her mind as she prepared to transition into a new phase of life.

Despite the uncertainty, Katelyn approached her retirement with a sense of gratitude. She reflected on the memories she had created, the friendships she had forged, and the lessons she had learned. Each competition, each practice, and each challenge had contributed to her growth, shaping her into the person she had become. While the thought of leaving gymnastics was bittersweet, Katelyn focused on celebrating the journey rather than mourning the end of an era.

Saying goodbye to gymnastics meant more than just stepping away from training and competition; it also involved bidding farewell to the routines and rituals that had become ingrained in her daily life. The early morning practices, the pre-competition nerves, and the camaraderie with teammates were experiences that had filled her days with purpose and joy. As she reflected on these moments, Katelyn recognized the significance of transition and the potential for new beginnings.

Retirement also opened the door to exploring interests and passions that had taken a backseat during her gymnastics career. Katelyn had always been passionate about sharing her story and advocating for body positivity and mental health awareness. With the time and space created by her retirement, she saw an opportunity to amplify her voice and connect with others on a broader scale. The decision to step away from gymnastics allowed her to engage in public speaking, workshops, and initiatives to empower young athletes and promote healthy body image.

Katelyn recognized that her experiences could resonate with many individuals navigating similar challenges. She hoped to inspire others to embrace their authenticity and prioritize their mental well-being by sharing her story. This newfound purpose filled her with excitement and motivation, providing a sense of direction as she transitioned from her role as a gymnast to an advocate and mentor.

As she navigated the emotional landscape of retirement, Katelyn also leaned on her support system. Friends, family, and mentors played a crucial role in helping her process the changes in her life. Their encouragement and understanding provided a safe space to express her fears and uncertainties. By sharing her feelings with those who had witnessed her journey, she found reassurance in the notion that retirement did not signify the end of her impact; rather, it was an evolution of her role as a leader in the athletic community.

The farewell to gymnastics was not just a personal journey; it also encompassed the relationships she had built within the sport. Katelyn understood that her retirement would affect her teammates, coaches, and fans. As she prepared to step away, she took the time to express her gratitude to those who had supported her throughout her career. Whether through heartfelt messages, personal conversations, or small gestures, Katelyn aimed to convey her appreciation for their collective journey.

Though retirement marked the end of one chapter, it also heralded the beginning of another. Katelyn envisioned a future filled with opportunities for growth and exploration. With a foundation built on resilience and dedication, she was eager to embrace new challenges in public speaking, advocacy work, or pursuing creative endeavors. This newfound freedom allowed her to redefine success on her terms, independent of the competitive structure that previously dictated her life.

As Katelyn transitioned from gymnastics, she maintained a sense of connection to the sport. While no longer competed, she remained an integral part of the gymnastics community. Whether through coaching, mentoring young athletes, or engaging with fans on social media, Katelyn recognized the importance of staying involved. Her experiences in gymnastics had shaped her identity, and she was determined to continue supporting the next generation of gymnasts. Retirement from gymnastics was a journey of self-discovery and transformation. Katelyn Ohashi embraced the complexities of leaving behind a sport she loved while opening herself to new experiences and opportunities. Her journey illustrated the resilience of the human spirit and the capacity to grow beyond the confines of a single identity. By sharing her story, Katelyn hoped to inspire others to approach their transitions with courage and optimism, reminding them that every ending holds the potential for a new beginning. Through her advocacy, she continues to empower young athletes, emphasizing the importance of authenticity, self-acceptance, and a holistic approach to well-being, proving that the spirit of gymnastics lives on within her, even as she embarks on new adventures beyond the mat.

Exploring New Avenues

After stepping away from the intense demands of gymnastics, Katelyn Ohashi found herself at a crossroads, eager to explore new paths that would allow her to utilize her experiences and passions in meaningful ways. Transitioning from the mat to various platforms required introspection and a willingness to embrace uncertainty. As she reflected on her journey, it became evident that writing, public speaking, and advocacy work allowed her to connect with others while sharing her unique perspective.

Katelyn's journey into writing began as a natural extension of her personal experiences. Throughout her career as an elite gymnast, she kept journals filled with her thoughts, feelings, and reflections on the triumphs and challenges she encountered. This practice became a source of comfort, allowing her to process her emotions and articulate her journey. With the transition into retirement, Katelyn felt compelled to share her story with a broader audience. She began crafting essays and articles that explored her experiences, particularly focusing on topics such as body image, mental health, and the pressures young athletes face. Writing became a form of self-expression and a means of reaching out to those who might feel isolated or misunderstood.

As she honed her writing skills, Katelyn discovered a talent for storytelling. Her ability to articulate complex emotions authentically and relatable resonated with many readers. The response to her writing was overwhelmingly positive, with individuals from various backgrounds expressing gratitude for her vulnerability and honesty. Katelyn recognized that her words had the power to inspire and uplift others, igniting her passion for writing further. Crafting narratives allowed her to reflect on her experiences, helping her make sense of her journey while encouraging others to embrace their unique stories.

Public speaking became another avenue for Katelyn to share her message and connect with audiences. Initially, speaking in front of large crowds filled her with excitement and apprehension. However, her performing background provided a sense of familiarity with being in the spotlight. Drawing on her experiences as a gymnast, she found ways to channel her nerves into a passionate delivery. Katelyn began participating in speaking engagements, addressing topics close to her heart. Whether sharing her journey through gymnastics, discussing the importance of mental health, or advocating for body positivity, her talks resonated with audiences eager to hear her story.

In addition to sharing her personal experiences, Katelyn emphasized the need for athletes to prioritize mental health. Drawing from her struggles, she highlighted the pressures that come with high-performance sports and the often-overlooked emotional toll. Her willingness to speak candidly about mental health fostered a sense of community among athletes, encouraging them to seek help and support when needed. As she traveled to schools, conferences, and workshops, Katelyn created a space where athletes could openly discuss their challenges, reinforcing that vulnerability is a strength rather than a weakness.

Advocacy work became an integral part of Katelyn's post-gymnastics journey. She recognized that her platform as a former elite gymnast could be leveraged to effect positive change in the lives of others. Partnering with organizations focused on mental health, body positivity, and youth empowerment, Katelyn became a vocal advocate for issues that matter deeply to her. Whether collaborating on campaigns or participating in initiatives to support young athletes, she approached her advocacy with purpose and determination.

Katelyn's advocacy efforts extended beyond the athletic community. She became involved in discussions surrounding unrealistic beauty standards perpetuated by media and society. Drawing from her own experiences with body image struggles, Katelyn sought to challenge harmful narratives that often surround athletes, particularly female athletes. Her message was clear: everybody is unique, and beauty comes in various forms. Through social media platforms and public appearances, she encouraged individuals to embrace their bodies, celebrating diversity and self-acceptance.

The creative process of writing, speaking, and advocating provided Katelyn with a sense of fulfillment that transcended the accolades she had earned as a gymnast. While her past was undeniably significant, the present and future excited her most. Engaging with individuals inspired by her journey brought a renewed sense of purpose as she witnessed firsthand the impact of her words and actions.

As Katelyn continued to explore these new avenues, she also recognized the importance of self-care and balance. The transition from athlete to advocate required her to be intentional about her well-being. Navigating the demands of writing, public speaking, and advocacy work could be overwhelming, especially as she adjusted to her new identity outside of gymnastics. To maintain her mental health, Katelyn established routines that included moments of reflection, physical activity, and connection with loved ones. These practices grounded her and fueled her passion for her work.

Throughout her journey, Katelyn found herself continually evolving. Each speaking engagement, every article she penned, and each conversation she had reinforced her commitment to authenticity. As she navigated the landscape of writing and advocacy, she remained dedicated to amplifying the voices of others who might feel unheard. Katelyn understood that her journey was about her personal story and creating a space for dialogue and empowerment.

In exploring new avenues, Katelyn Ohashi transformed her retirement from gymnastics into an opportunity for growth and connection. Writing allowed her to articulate her experiences and foster understanding among readers, while public speaking provided a platform to inspire and encourage others. Through advocacy, she became a champion for mental health awareness and body positivity, addressing issues that resonate deeply with individuals of all backgrounds.

As she embraced this new chapter, Katelyn's journey served as a reminder that change can be both challenging and rewarding. The lessons she learned as a gymnast continued to inform her approach to advocacy and writing, emphasizing resilience, determination, and the importance of embracing one's authentic self. Through her dedication to creating positive change, Katelyn Ohashi emerged not only as a former gymnast but also as a powerful advocate and voice for a generation of young athletes seeking guidance and inspiration. Her journey underscored the idea that life after sports can be a rich and fulfilling experience, where every new avenue explored contributes to the broader narrative of self-discovery and empowerment.

Adjusting to Life Without Elite Competition

Transitioning away from elite gymnastics marked a significant turning point for Katelyn Ohashi, a moment laden with challenges and opportunities. The adrenaline-fueled life of a competitive athlete had defined her existence for years, shaping her physical capabilities and identity. As she stepped back from the rigorous demands of training and competition, she faced redefining herself in a world no longer dominated by the beam and the floor.

Initially, the absence of daily practices, competitions, and teammates' camaraderie left a difficult void to navigate. The routines that had structured her life became memories; without them, Katelyn experienced feelings of loss. This shift demanded an adjustment that was both emotional and practical. The life she had once known, filled with the thrill of performances and the pursuit of perfection, transformed into something uncertain and undefined.

To cope with this transition, Katelyn leaned on her support system, friends, family, and mentors who had been part of her journey. They provided a sense of continuity, reminding her of the strength and resilience that had propelled her through countless competitions. Conversations with those who understood her struggles helped to validate her feelings and reassure her that it was normal to experience such a significant change. This support became a cornerstone in her adjustment process, as it offered a sense of belonging in a new and overwhelming world.

Amid the emotional upheaval, Katelyn began to explore activities that had previously piqued her interest but had taken a backseat to her gymnastics career. She discovered a passion for writing, an outlet that allowed her to articulate her experiences and share her story with others. Crafting essays and articles became a therapeutic practice, enabling her to reflect on her journey and connect with readers who resonated with her struggles and triumphs. Writing was not just a creative endeavor; it became a way for Katelyn to process her thoughts, revealing layers of her identity that the demands of sport had overshadowed.

With each word she penned, Katelyn found a new rhythm, one that was distinctly different from the precise movements of gymnastics. This new pursuit allowed her to express herself authentically and liberally. She began to see her writing as a means of storytelling and a bridge to engage with wider conversations about mental health, body positivity, and the realities athletes face. It provided her with a platform to advocate for issues close to her heart, giving her a renewed sense of purpose.

Exploring her passion for writing opened doors to other creative outlets. Katelyn found joy in photography, capturing moments of beauty and emotion that resonated with her experiences. The lens offered a different perspective, allowing her to freeze time and explore the world through a new filter. Photography became an extension of her storytelling, adding a visual layer to her narratives. Whether she was documenting her travels, sharing candid moments with friends, or exploring her surroundings, each snapshot reflected her evolving identity and the beauty of her new life beyond gymnastics.

As Katelyn embraced these new passions, she also sought opportunities to stay active, recognizing the importance of physical movement in maintaining her well-being. The intensity of gymnastics may have receded, but her love for movement remained. She experimented with various forms of exercise, from yoga and dance to hiking and fitness classes. Each new experience brought a sense of discovery, allowing her to reconnect with her body differently. Katelyn relished the freedom to engage in physical activities without the pressures of competition looming over her.

Alongside her creative pursuits and active lifestyle, Katelyn began to explore opportunities for public speaking and advocacy. Drawing on her experiences as an athlete, she became passionate about sharing her story with others, particularly young athletes grappling with similar challenges. Speaking engagements allowed her to connect with audiences in a fulfilling and impactful way. Her talks emphasized the importance of mental health, resilience, and embracing one's unique journey. This new role as a speaker empowered her and reminded her of the lessons she had learned throughout her gymnastics career.

Finding her footing beyond elite competition also involved cultivating new friendships and connections. As she moved away from the gymnastics community, Katelyn sought to build relationships with individuals who shared her writing, advocacy, and creativity interests. Engaging with like-minded individuals brought a refreshing energy into her life, fostering a sense of camaraderie and support. These new friendships encouraged her to step outside her comfort zone and explore new experiences, enriching her journey of self-discovery.

Katelyn soon realized that adjusting to life after gymnastics was not just about replacing one passion with another; it was about embracing the fullness of her identity. The lessons she had learned through gymnastics, such as discipline, perseverance, and the value of hard work, remained relevant in every new endeavor she pursued. As she faced the inevitable ups and downs of adjusting to a new lifestyle, Katelyn drew on these core principles to navigate challenges, reminding herself that growth often comes from discomfort.

Throughout her journey, moments of self-reflection became essential. Katelyn took time to evaluate her values, aspirations, and what truly brought her joy. This introspection allowed her to clarify her goals and develop a vision for her future. Rather than feeling lost without gymnastics, she began to see the possibilities ahead. Each day became an opportunity to explore her passions, whether through writing, speaking, or pursuing creative projects that ignited her spirit.

As the months passed, Katelyn's confidence grew. The initial uncertainties gradually transformed into a sense of empowerment. She began to embrace her new identity as an advocate for mental health and body positivity, recognizing the importance of her voice in inspiring others. The challenges she faced during her transition became a source of strength, reinforcing her commitment to authenticity and self-acceptance. Katelyn understood that her journey was unique and that it was okay to carve out a new path, free from the constraints of competition.

In this discovery process, Katelyn Ohashi emerged as a former elite gymnast and a multifaceted individual with many interests and passions. She learned to navigate life with a newfound sense of purpose, embracing the complexities of her identity beyond gymnastics. The journey of adjusting to life without elite competition transformed from a daunting task into a vibrant exploration of creativity, advocacy, and self-acceptance.

The lessons learned during her gymnastics career became the foundation for Katelyn's new life. The pursuit of excellence shifted from the mat to personal growth, reminding her that the journey is as significant as the destination. Through writing, public speaking, and connecting with others, Katelyn found fulfillment in sharing her story while encouraging others to embrace their unique journeys. As she forged ahead, Katelyn Ohashi illuminated the path for those navigating similar transitions, showing that life after elite competition can be a canvas for endless possibilities and self-discovery.

Chapter 9: Impact on Gymnastics and Pop Culture

How Katelyn's Story Has Changed Gymnastics Culture

Katelyn Ohashi's journey through gymnastics has transcended the sport, sparking significant conversations about body image, mental health, and the culture surrounding athletes. Her story, particularly following her viral routine that captured the hearts of millions, became a catalyst for change, challenging long-standing norms and pushing for a more inclusive and compassionate environment within gymnastics and beyond.

One of the most striking aspects of Katelyn's impact is her open discussion regarding body positivity and self-acceptance. Historically, gymnastics has been plagued by strict beauty standards prioritizing appearance over athleticism. Katelyn's rise to fame has highlighted the importance of embracing one's body as it is rather than conforming to an often unrealistic ideal. Through her platform, she has inspired countless young athletes to challenge societal expectations, promoting that self-worth should not be measured by body size or shape. Katelyn's commitment to body positivity has resonated deeply with gymnasts who have felt pressured to fit a certain mold, encouraging them to celebrate their individuality and unique physical attributes.

Moreover, Katelyn's candidness about her struggles with body image and mental health has opened the door for crucial conversations that were previously sidelined in the world of sports. Athletes have felt compelled to maintain a façade of perfection for many years, often hiding their vulnerabilities and insecurities. Katelyn's willingness to share her experiences has created a ripple effect, encouraging other gymnasts and athletes to speak out about their challenges. This cultural shift has fostered an environment where mental health is prioritized, and athletes feel more supported in seeking help and expressing their emotions. Her story has contributed to a broader understanding that mental well-being is as important as physical performance, paving the way for more resources and conversations around mental health in gymnastics and other sports.

In addition to her advocacy for body positivity and mental health awareness, Katelyn's influence has extended to how gymnastics is perceived in popular culture. Her viral floor routine, characterized by creativity, joy, and personality, showcased gymnastics as an art form beyond technical precision. This moment captivated audiences and redefined what success looks like in the sport. Katelyn's emphasis on enjoyment and self-expression has encouraged a generation of gymnasts to prioritize their love for the sport over the pressures of competition. By showcasing gymnastics' fun and artistic side, she has helped shift the narrative, reminding athletes and fans alike that gymnastics can express joy rather than solely pursue perfection.

Katelyn's influence has also sparked discussions among coaches, parents, and organizations about pressure on young athletes. Many individuals involved in gymnastics have begun to reassess training methods, emphasizing the importance of nurturing an athlete's overall well-being rather than solely focusing on results. This cultural change has encouraged a more holistic approach to coaching, where the athlete's mental, emotional, and physical health takes precedence. Katelyn's story has prompted conversations about creating a supportive environment where athletes can thrive without succumbing to the overwhelming pressures historically defining the sport.

The impact of Katelyn's journey has also reached the broader community of women in sports. As she has taken a stand against unrealistic beauty standards and the stigma surrounding mental health, her story has resonated with athletes across various disciplines. Many female athletes have drawn strength from Katelyn's authenticity, inspiring them to share their stories and advocate for change in their respective sports. The solidarity fostered by Katelyn's bravery in speaking out has encouraged a collective movement toward a culture of empowerment, where female athletes uplift one another and advocate for their rights and well-being.

Katelyn's activism extends beyond her own experiences. She has utilized her platform to advocate for systemic changes within gymnastics organizations, urging them to implement policies prioritizing athlete safety and mental health. By addressing issues such as body shaming, harassment, and the need for comprehensive mental health resources, Katelyn has become a powerful voice for athletes who may feel voiceless. Her commitment to enacting change has inspired others to join her cause, leading to a growing movement to reshape the gymnastics culture.

Through her advocacy work, Katelyn has inspired a new generation of gymnasts to approach their sport with empowerment and confidence. The conversations sparked by her story have encouraged young athletes to prioritize their well-being, seek support, and advocate for change when necessary. As Katelyn continues to share her journey, she reinforces the idea that it is not just about achieving perfection in competition but also about nurturing one's mental health, self-acceptance, and love for the sport.

The transformation of gymnastics culture, partly due to Katelyn's influence, signals a significant shift toward a more inclusive and supportive environment. Athletes are now more vocal about their experiences, and organizations increasingly recognize the need for policies that protect and empower athletes. This shift signifies a departure from the rigid expectations of the past, embracing a more compassionate approach that values individuality, mental health, and the overall well-being of athletes.

As Katelyn Ohashi continues her journey beyond gymnastics, her story serves as a reminder that change is possible through vulnerability, courage, and advocacy. By bravely sharing her experiences, she has illuminated a path for others to follow, encouraging them to embrace their authentic selves and advocate for their rights. The cultural shift she has inspired within gymnastics and the wider sports community emphasizes the importance of empathy, support, and understanding in fostering a healthier environment for athletes of all backgrounds.

Katelyn's story has undeniably changed gymnastics culture, encouraging a movement toward body positivity, mental health awareness, and a redefinition of success. Her impact extends beyond the competition floor, reaching young athletes, coaches, and organizations, fostering a community that values well-being, individuality, and self-acceptance. As more athletes feel empowered to share their stories and advocate for change, the legacy of Katelyn Ohashi's journey will continue to inspire future generations to embrace their uniqueness and redefine what it means to be a successful athlete.

The Shift in Media Representation of Female Athletes

The representation of female athletes in the media has undergone a profound transformation over the past few decades. Historically, coverage often focused on appearances rather than achievements, reducing accomplished sportswomen to mere figures that fit stereotypical molds. However, a gradual yet impactful shift has emerged, as athletes like Katelyn Ohashi have brought visibility to issues surrounding body image, self-acceptance, and the narrative of female athleticism. This evolution reflects a change in how female athletes are portrayed and a growing awareness of the importance of diverse representation within the sports world.

In earlier eras, media narratives often emphasized the physical attributes of female athletes, frequently prioritizing aesthetics over athletic prowess. This trend perpetuated unrealistic standards of beauty and fueled a culture of body shaming, where success was measured by a woman's ability to conform to societal ideals. Gymnasts, in particular, faced immense pressure to maintain a certain physique, which often overshadowed their remarkable skills and hard work. Such representation created an environment where female athletes struggled to gain recognition for their talents, as the media spotlight focused on their looks rather than their accomplishments.

The tide began to turn as a new generation of female athletes emerged, unafraid to challenge the status quo. Katelyn Ohashi's viral routine was a watershed moment, showcasing her technical skills, vitality, and joy in performing. This routine, which garnered millions of views and widespread acclaim, highlighted the need for a shift in focus from how female athletes look to what they can achieve. The media's enthusiastic embrace of Katelyn's performance marked a pivotal point in how female athletes were covered, reflecting a broader movement toward recognizing their capabilities and contributions to their sports.

As social media platforms gained popularity, they provided female athletes a direct avenue to share their narratives and connect with audiences on their terms. No longer reliant solely on traditional media outlets, these athletes began to craft their images, showcasing their skills, training regimens, and personal stories. The power of social media allowed them to highlight not just their physical appearances but also their journeys, struggles, and triumphs. Katelyn and her peers utilized these platforms to create a more authentic representation of themselves, demonstrating that athletes are multifaceted individuals with diverse experiences beyond their sport.

The change in media representation has also been fueled by a growing movement advocating for body positivity and mental health awareness among athletes. Conversations about the pressures female athletes face regarding body image have gained momentum, thanks in part to figures like Katelyn, who have openly discussed their struggles. This new focus on mental well-being and self-acceptance has encouraged media outlets to adopt a more nuanced approach when covering female athletes, moving beyond surface-level observations to highlight their resilience and strength.

Additionally, the increased visibility of female athletes in various sports has contributed to a more inclusive narrative. Once considered male-dominated, sports now see female athletes receive recognition for their talents. This shift in representation reflects a broader societal change toward valuing equality and diversity. Media coverage has expanded to include stories of female athletes breaking barriers, challenging stereotypes, and achieving extraordinary feats. The stories now celebrate female athletes' diverse backgrounds, experiences, and aspirations, allowing them to be recognized as trailblazers in their respective sports.

However, challenges remain in achieving full representation and equity in media coverage. Despite the progress made, female athletes still often fight for equal visibility, particularly in comparison to their male counterparts. The disparities in coverage frequency and the depth of stories highlight the need for continued advocacy. Female athletes like Katelyn Ohashi are essential in this movement, as they excel in their sports and use their platforms to amplify the voices of their peers and advocate for systemic change within the industry.

Media outlets play a crucial role in shaping public perceptions of female athletes, and there is a growing expectation that they move beyond traditional narratives that focus solely on appearance. As audiences demand more comprehensive coverage, sports journalism has an opportunity to embrace a more diverse set of stories. By highlighting female athletes' accomplishments, struggles, and personal growth, the media can help reshape the narrative and challenge longstanding stereotypes.

The impact of Katelyn Ohashi's journey extends beyond her personal experiences. Her story has inspired countless female athletes to embrace their identities and reject the notion that they must conform to narrow beauty standards. This newfound confidence encourages young athletes to pursue their dreams while remaining true to themselves. As more athletes enter the spotlight and share their authentic stories, the media will be compelled to adapt and reflect the rich tapestry of experiences that characterize female athletics.

Katelyn's influence has also prompted discussions within sports organizations about the importance of diverse representation. As female athletes advocate for their rights and call for equitable treatment, it is essential for governing bodies and sponsors to recognize the value of elevating women's sports. This recognition must translate into increased investment in female athletes, more opportunities for visibility, and a commitment to creating environments where female athletes can thrive both on and off the field.

The shift in media representation is not just a trend but a critical evolution that holds the potential to shape the future of women's sports. As the narrative continues to shift toward celebrating the accomplishments and experiences of female athletes, all stakeholders must engage in meaningful conversations about representation and inclusivity. The journey toward equitable coverage is ongoing, but the strides made thus far indicate a growing recognition of the need for change.

As we look to the future, the stories of female athletes like Katelyn Ohashi will be a powerful reminder of the importance of authenticity, resilience, and courage. Their journeys inspire fellow athletes and a broader audience that seeks to challenge societal norms and celebrate diversity. With each story told, the potential for change increases, paving the way for future generations to thrive in an environment that values their contributions, empowers their voices, and embraces their unique identities.

The ongoing evolution of media representation of female athletes reflects a profound cultural shift toward recognizing the value of diversity, authenticity, and empowerment. Katelyn Ohashi's journey exemplifies the power of an individual voice in fostering change, inspiring her peers and the next generation of athletes to embrace their true selves and redefine what it means to succeed in sports. As this narrative continues to evolve, the possibilities for female athletes are limitless, ensuring that their stories will be celebrated and valued for years to come.

Her Lasting Legacy

Katelyn Ohashi's impact on the world of gymnastics and beyond is marked by her unique blend of joy, authenticity, and empowerment. Her legacy is not merely one of athletic achievements; it profoundly influences how young athletes perceive themselves and the expectations placed upon them. Through her vibrant performances and candid discussions about self-acceptance, Katelyn has ignited a movement that celebrates individuality and encourages others to embrace their true selves. This legacy is a testament to the power of authenticity in sports and the importance of joy in pursuing excellence.

From the moment Katelyn burst onto the scene with her infectious personality and captivating routines, it was clear that she was more than just another gymnast. Her performances radiated a sense of joy that was often missing in the highly competitive world of gymnastics, where pressure and expectations can overshadow the pure love of the sport. Katelyn approached each routine as an opportunity to express herself, infusing her performances with fun and creativity that resonated with audiences worldwide. Her enthusiasm transformed the experience of watching gymnastics into a celebration of movement rather than just a display of technical skill.

This celebration of joy did not come without its challenges. Katelyn faced significant pressure to conform to traditional expectations of what a gymnast should look like and how she should perform. The gymnastics community has historically been characterized by rigid standards regarding body types and techniques, often sidelining the individuality of the athletes. Yet, Katelyn remained steadfast in her commitment to authenticity. She understood that gymnastics while demanding precision and discipline, should also allow for personal expression and creativity. By staying true to herself, Katelyn redefined her own experience in the sport and paved the way for others to follow.

Her journey took a pivotal turn with the viral success of her floor routine, showcasing her impressive skills while celebrating her personality. Millions were captivated by her athletic prowess and ability to connect with the audience through her performances. This moment marked a significant cultural shift, demonstrating that joy and authenticity could coexist with excellence. Katelyn's routine was not just a performance; it was a declaration that gymnastics could be a source of happiness and self-expression, challenging the notion that success must come at the expense of joy.

Katelyn's courage to be herself resonated with many young athletes grappling with the pressures of competition. She became a beacon of hope for those overwhelmed by unrealistic standards imposed on them by coaches, parents, and society. Through her candid discussions about body image and mental health, Katelyn opened the door for important conversations about athletes' struggles. She has bravely shared her own experiences with body shaming and the emotional toll it can take, creating a safe space for others to speak out about their challenges. Her willingness to be vulnerable has fostered a sense of community among athletes, encouraging them to support one another and prioritize their mental well-being.

As Katelyn transitioned away from competitive gymnastics, her influence did not wane; instead, it expanded into new avenues of advocacy and empowerment. She has become a prominent voice in discussions about body positivity and mental health, using her platform to champion the importance of self-acceptance. Katelyn's message extends far beyond the gymnastics floor; it speaks to the heart of what it means to be an athlete in today's world. She emphasizes that each person's journey is unique and that embracing individuality is key to finding happiness and fulfillment in sports.

Katelyn's empowerment is reflected in the countless young athletes who look up to her. They see not just a talented gymnast but a role model who demonstrates that success can be redefined. Katelyn encourages these athletes to pursue their passions without fear of judgment or the need to conform to societal expectations. Her influence shapes a new generation of athletes who value joy, authenticity, and personal growth over superficial achievements. This shift is profound, as it departs from the traditional narratives that have long dominated sports culture.

Katelyn's legacy of empowerment through joy and authenticity is evident in her initiatives beyond gymnastics. As a public speaker and advocate, she shares her story with diverse audiences, inspiring individuals from all walks of life. Whether speaking to young athletes, mental health organizations, or community groups, Katelyn emphasizes the importance of being true to oneself. Her resilience, positivity, and self-love resonate deeply, encouraging others to embrace their identities and pursue their dreams fearlessly.

Moreover, her impact on gymnastics culture unfolds as more athletes step into the spotlight, inspired by Katelyn's example. They are beginning to realize that their stories matter and that their voices can effect change. The gymnastics community is slowly becoming a more inclusive space where diversity is celebrated and individuality is encouraged. This cultural transformation reflects the legacy that Katelyn has built, one where joy is not just allowed but prioritized.

The power of Katelyn's story lies in its universality. While she is known primarily for her gymnastics achievements, her journey's themes resonate with anyone facing the pressures of conformity. Her emphasis on self-acceptance and joy is a call to action for individuals of all ages and backgrounds. In a world often filled with negativity and comparison, Katelyn's message shines brightly, reminding us that embracing who we are is a powerful act of defiance against societal norms.

Katelyn Ohashi's lasting legacy celebrates empowerment through joy and authenticity. Her journey is a reminder that success in sports and in life should not be measured solely by trophies or accolades. Instead, it should encompass the joy of pursuing one's passions and the courage to be oneself. Katelyn's influence will continue to inspire young athletes for generations to come, encouraging them to redefine what it means to succeed on their terms. The world of gymnastics and beyond is richer for her contributions, and her story will forever be a beacon of hope for those navigating the complexities of self-identity and achievement.

Chapter 10: The Ongoing Journey

Continuing Her Advocacy for Mental Health and Body Image

Katelyn Ohashi's journey as an athlete transcends the confines of gymnastics, evolving into a powerful advocacy for mental health and body image awareness. After stepping away from elite competition, Katelyn recognized that her platform could be utilized to address issues that resonated deeply within the sports community and beyond. Her experiences have not only shaped her understanding of the importance of mental health but have also propelled her to become a voice for those who struggle silently with similar challenges.

Throughout her competitive career, Katelyn grappled with the pressures of perfection often imposed on gymnasts. The sport is notorious for emphasizing physical appearance alongside technical prowess, leading many athletes to develop unhealthy relationships with their bodies. Katelyn's own experiences with body image struggles made her acutely aware of the toll such pressures can take on young athletes, many of whom feel they must conform to unrealistic standards to gain acceptance and recognition. This awareness ignited a passion within her to champion a more inclusive and compassionate narrative surrounding body image in sports.

As Katelyn began to speak openly about her struggles, she became a source of inspiration for many. Her willingness to share her story allowed others to see they were not alone in their experiences. By discussing her battles with body shaming and the anxiety that often accompanied competition, Katelyn humanized the challenges faced by athletes. She emphasized that mental health should be prioritized and that acknowledging one's vulnerabilities is not a sign of weakness but rather an act of strength. This shift in perspective resonated with individuals who had previously felt isolated in their struggles.

Katelyn has taken her advocacy to various platforms, using social media as a powerful tool to reach a wide audience. Her posts often include messages about self-acceptance, body positivity, and the importance of mental well-being. She shares her insights through candid reflections and motivational content, encouraging her followers to embrace their unique journeys. By addressing her vulnerabilities, Katelyn fosters a culture of openness, urging her audience to break the silence surrounding mental health issues and to seek help when needed.

One of the most significant aspects of Katelyn's advocacy is her emphasis on redefining beauty standards within sports. She challenges the notion that athletes must conform to a particular body type to be successful. Katelyn frequently highlights the importance of celebrating diverse body shapes and sizes, asserting that athleticism comes in many forms. Her advocacy encourages athletes to recognize their strengths and capabilities rather than focusing solely on external appearances. This shift can potentially revolutionize how young athletes view themselves and their bodies, fostering a healthier, more positive environment in competitive sports.

Katelyn's involvement extends beyond social media; she actively engages in speaking events, panels, and workshops on mental health and body image. These engagements allow her to share her story more personally and effectively. During these talks, Katelyn emphasizes the importance of mental health resources for athletes, advocating for a culture that prioritizes emotional well-being. She works to bridge the gap between athletics and mental health support by collaborating with mental health organizations and participating in community initiatives.

In her advocacy, Katelyn also highlights the role of coaches and mentors in shaping the experiences of young athletes. She encourages coaches to foster an environment where mental health is openly discussed, normalizing conversations around anxiety, stress, and self-worth. Katelyn believes that when coaches prioritize emotional well-being alongside performance, they empower athletes to express themselves authentically. This holistic approach can lead to more resilient athletes better equipped to handle the pressures of competition.

The impact of Katelyn's advocacy is evident in the growing conversations around mental health in sports. As more athletes feel empowered to share their struggles, the stigma surrounding mental health begins to dissolve. Katelyn's influence has encouraged many to seek help and advocate for themselves and their peers. She has become a catalyst for change, inspiring a new generation of athletes to prioritize their mental health as they pursue their passions.

Katelyn has also collaborated with various organizations focused on mental health and wellness, providing her voice to initiatives that align with her values. By partnering with these groups, she helps create resources and programs to support athletes in navigating the complexities of mental health. Her involvement raises awareness and provides tangible support to those who may be struggling.

The impact of Katelyn's work can be seen in the positive changes occurring within the sports community. More athletes are beginning to prioritize their mental health, recognizing that it is integral to their overall well-being. The narrative is shifting toward one that values emotional health alongside physical performance, fostering a culture where athletes can thrive mentally and physically.

As Katelyn continues her advocacy journey, she remains dedicated to amplifying the voices of those who have been marginalized or silenced. She believes that everyone deserves the right to feel confident in their bodies and to prioritize their mental health without fear of judgment. Through her ongoing efforts, Katelyn aims to create a legacy that transforms the gymnastics culture and inspires athletes from all disciplines to advocate for themselves and others.

Katelyn Ohashi's commitment to mental health and body image advocacy reflects her belief in the power of authenticity. By sharing her story and experiences, she encourages others to embrace their true selves, fostering an environment where vulnerability is celebrated. Her journey serves as a reminder that athletes are more than just their achievements; they are individuals with feelings, struggles, and dreams. Katelyn's advocacy is not just about changing perceptions within sports but empowering individuals to reclaim their narratives and find strength in their authenticity.

The road ahead is bright as Katelyn champions cause close to her heart. Her work is a testament to the resilience of the human spirit and the transformative power of vulnerability. As she forges new paths in advocacy, she inspires countless others to join the movement toward mental health awareness and body positivity, ensuring that her legacy will continue to impact future generations. Katelyn's story is one of courage, empowerment, and unwavering commitment to creating a world where all individuals can feel accepted and valued for who they truly are.

Lessons Learned from Her Journey

Katelyn Ohashi's journey through gymnastics has been a tapestry woven with experiences that have shaped her into a powerful advocate for mental health and body positivity. As she transitioned from an elite athlete to a public figure and speaker, she encountered various challenges that provided her profound insights into herself and the world around her. The lessons learned from her experiences are personal and personal and resonate with many who face their battles in pursuit of their passions.

One of the most significant lessons Katelyn learned is the importance of self-acceptance. Throughout her gymnastics career, she faced intense scrutiny regarding her performance and appearance. The pressures of competition often led her to internalize criticism, making her feel that she needed to conform to specific standards to be valued. This struggle with self-acceptance became a pivotal point in her life, leading her to recognize the futility of seeking validation from others. Katelyn found freedom and empowerment by embracing her individuality and recognizing her worth independent of external opinions. This journey of self-acceptance became a core theme in her advocacy, encouraging others to celebrate their uniqueness.

Another critical lesson emerged from her experiences with mental health. Katelyn grappled with anxiety and the overwhelming pressures of performing at a high level. These challenges highlighted the importance of mental well-being, prompting her to prioritize her emotional health over societal expectations. Katelyn realized that vulnerability is not a weakness but a strength that connects people. Sharing her struggles openly allowed her to break down barriers and create a dialogue about mental health in sports. This understanding transformed her relationship with performance, enabling her to approach competitions with a healthier mindset.

The journey through gymnastics also taught Katelyn the significance of resilience. The sport demands a high level of physical and mental endurance, often requiring athletes to push through injuries, setbacks, and moments of self-doubt. Katelyn experienced her fair share of obstacles, but instead of succumbing to despair, she learned to view these challenges as opportunities for growth. Each setback became a lesson, reinforcing her belief that perseverance is essential. This resilience fueled her athletic success and became a guiding principle in her life after gymnastics. She now encourages others to cultivate resilience, reminding them that it is through adversity that strength is forged.

Katelyn's journey also revealed the importance of community and support. She encountered individuals who believed in her throughout her career, offering encouragement and guidance during difficult times. Whether it was her family, coaches, or teammates, these relationships played a crucial role in her development as an athlete and a person. Recognizing the impact of these connections, Katelyn emphasizes the need for a supportive environment, particularly in sports. She advocates for athletes to lean on one another and seek help when needed, fostering a culture of camaraderie that uplifts everyone involved. Athletes can navigate their challenges more resiliently by building a strong support system.

Moreover, Katelyn learned the significance of using her platform for advocacy. As she transitioned from an athlete to a public figure, she recognized that her experiences could inspire change. Katelyn became passionate about addressing issues such as body image and mental health, realizing that her voice could resonate with others who faced similar struggles. This shift in perspective empowered her to speak out against unrealistic beauty standards and promote body positivity. Katelyn now encourages others to use their platforms to advocate for causes that matter to them, regardless of how large or small. Individuals can effect change in their communities and beyond by amplifying important conversations.

Her journey also reinforced the idea that personal growth is a continuous process. Katelyn acknowledges that the path to self-discovery and empowerment is not linear but filled with ups and downs. Each experience, whether positive or negative, contributes to her evolution as a person. Katelyn encourages individuals to embrace their journeys, understanding that growth often occurs in the face of challenges. She advocates for a mindset that embraces learning and adaptation, allowing people to navigate life's complexities with grace and resilience.

Additionally, Katelyn discovered the power of storytelling as a means of connection. Sharing her experiences and vulnerabilities opened doors for conversations that might not have happened otherwise. She created a space for others to do the same by being authentic and transparent about her struggles. Katelyn emphasizes sharing stories through social media, speaking engagements, or personal interactions. These narratives can foster empathy, understanding, and solidarity among individuals facing similar challenges. Katelyn believes that when people share their stories, they contribute to a collective healing process that benefits everyone involved.

The lessons Katelyn learned extend beyond her journey; they have the potential to impact the broader cultural landscape of gymnastics and sports as a whole. Her advocacy for mental health awareness and body positivity encourages athletes to redefine their relationship with their bodies and performance. Katelyn's message challenges the notion that accolades and appearances solely define success. Instead, she promotes a holistic approach that values mental and emotional well-being alongside physical achievement. This shift in perspective is vital in creating a healthier environment for future generations of athletes.

Moreover, Katelyn's journey underscores the importance of authenticity in sports. She emphasizes that athletes should not feel pressured to fit into predefined molds but rather be encouraged to express their true selves. This authenticity resonates deeply with fans and aspiring athletes, fostering a culture of acceptance where individuals can thrive without fear of judgment. Katelyn advocates for a shift in the narrative surrounding athletes, urging the sports community to celebrate diversity and individuality rather than conformity.

Katelyn Ohashi's journey through gymnastics is a testament to the power of personal growth. The lessons she learned continue to shape her advocacy work and inspire others to embark on their journeys of self-discovery. Katelyn's emphasis on self-acceptance, resilience, community support, and authenticity serves as a guiding light for those navigating the complexities of life. Her commitment to mental health awareness and body positivity reflects a desire to create a more inclusive and compassionate world for athletes and individuals from all walks of life. As Katelyn continues to share her story and advocate for meaningful change, she leaves an indelible mark on the hearts of those who can hear her message. Through her experiences, Katelyn reminds us that personal growth is not just a destination but a continuous journey of exploration, learning, and connection.

Katelyn's Vision for the Future and Her Role as a Changemaker

Katelyn Ohashi's vision for the future extends far beyond her days as an elite gymnast. Having emerged from the rigors of competition with a wealth of experience, she is driven by a desire to foster change in the world of sports and beyond. Her commitment to advocacy, particularly in mental health and body positivity, showcases her understanding of the challenges faced by athletes and the broader community. Katelyn recognizes the power of her platform to influence positive change and aims to utilize it to inspire others to join her mission.

At the heart of Katelyn's vision lies a deep-seated belief in the importance of mental well-being. Through her own experiences, she has seen firsthand the detrimental effects of performance pressure on mental health. The societal expectations placed on athletes, especially female athletes, can create an environment rife with anxiety and self-doubt. Katelyn is determined to shift this narrative, advocating for a culture where mental health is prioritized alongside physical performance. She envisions a future in which athletes feel empowered to speak openly about their mental health struggles without fear of stigma or retribution.

Katelyn's advocacy also emphasizes the need for comprehensive mental health resources within sports organizations. She believes that just as physical training is essential for athletic success, mental training should be equally prioritized. Her vision includes implementing programs that educate athletes on mental health awareness, coping strategies, and seeking help. By equipping athletes with the tools they need to navigate their mental health, Katelyn aims to create an environment where individuals can thrive both on and off the field.

Additionally, Katelyn is passionate about promoting body positivity and challenging the unrealistic beauty standards that have long permeated the sports world. She understands that these standards can lead to harmful behaviors and a negative self-image among athletes. Through her advocacy work, Katelyn encourages individuals to embrace their bodies in all forms and celebrate the strength and capability of being an athlete. Her message is clear: self-worth is not defined by appearance but rather by character, determination, and the impact one has on others.

In her vision for the future, Katelyn seeks to inspire a new generation of athletes to prioritize their health and authenticity. She wants young athletes to recognize that they do not have to conform to societal expectations to achieve success. By sharing her journey of self-discovery, Katelyn hopes to empower others to embrace their unique identities and pursue their passions fearlessly. She believes authenticity should be celebrated rather than stifled, creating a culture where athletes feel comfortable expressing their true selves. Katelyn also sees the importance of fostering a supportive community among athletes. She recognizes that an athlete's journey can often feel isolating, particularly when faced with challenges and setbacks. By encouraging collaboration and camaraderie among athletes, Katelyn envisions a future where individuals uplift one another rather than compete against each other in harmful ways. This sense of community is essential for promoting mental well-being and cultivating resilience.

Katelyn aims to create a ripple effect beyond individual athletes through her advocacy. She hopes to inspire coaches, parents, and sports organizations to adopt a more holistic approach to training and development. By prioritizing mental health and body positivity at all levels of sport, Katelyn envisions a transformation in the culture of athletics, one that values individuals for their contributions, efforts, and authenticity rather than mere performance metrics.

Katelyn is also committed to using her voice in the media to amplify these messages. She recognizes the power of storytelling in shaping public perception and influencing change. Through interviews, public speaking engagements, and social media platforms, Katelyn seeks to raise awareness about the issues that matter most to her. By sharing her experiences and insights, she aims to spark conversations that challenge the status quo and encourage others to engage in advocacy work.

Looking ahead, Katelyn sees herself as an advocate and a changemaker within the sports community. She aspires to collaborate with organizations dedicated to mental health awareness and body positivity, developing initiatives that create lasting impact. Whether through workshops, campaigns, or partnerships, Katelyn envisions a future where her efforts contribute to a more inclusive and supportive environment for all athletes.

Katelyn's vision also extends to the broader society, recognizing that the issues she champions are not confined to sports. Body image concerns and mental health challenges are pervasive across various demographics and industries. Using her platform to advocate for positive change, Katelyn aims to influence societal perceptions and encourage a cultural shift toward acceptance and compassion. She envisions a future where individuals are celebrated for their diversity, resilience, and authenticity rather than judged by arbitrary standards.

As she continues to navigate her post-gymastics career, Katelyn remains committed to lifelong learning and growth. She recognizes that the journey of advocacy is ongoing and that each experience contributes to her understanding of the complexities surrounding mental health and body image. By remaining open to new perspectives and experiences, Katelyn aims to refine her approach to advocacy, ensuring that her efforts are informed and impactful.

Katelyn Ohashi's vision for the future is rooted in hope and determination. She believes in the potential for change within the world of sports and society. Through her advocacy work, she aims to empower individuals to embrace their true selves, prioritize their mental well-being, and challenge the unrealistic standards imposed upon them. Katelyn's role as a changemaker is not just about raising awareness but about inspiring action and creating a legacy that transcends her own experiences.

Katelyn envisions a future where athletes feel free to express themselves and thrive by fostering a culture of authenticity, resilience, and support. Her journey has equipped her with invaluable insights, and she is poised to use them to inspire meaningful change. With each step she takes, Katelyn paves the way for a brighter future, where individuals are empowered to embrace their identities, prioritize their well-being, and impact the world around them.

CONCLUSION

Katelyn Ohashi's journey transcends the boundaries of sport, embodying a profound narrative of resilience, advocacy, and personal growth. Through her experiences in gymnastics, she has illuminated critical issues related to mental health and body image, creating a significant impact that resonates far beyond the gymnastics community. Her story is a powerful reminder of the importance of authenticity, courage, and self-acceptance in a world often dominated by unrealistic expectations and societal pressures.

Throughout this book, we have explored the multifaceted aspects of Katelyn's life and career, from her triumphs as an elite athlete to her courageous stand against the pressures often accompanying such a role. Her advocacy for body positivity and mental health has positioned her as a trailblazer, inspiring countless individuals to challenge the standards imposed upon them. Katelyn's willingness to share her struggles and triumphs has fostered an environment where open dialogue about mental health is not only accepted but celebrated.

The lessons from Katelyn's experiences are invaluable for aspiring athletes and individuals. Her emphasis on prioritizing mental health alongside physical training highlights the need for a comprehensive approach to well-being in sports. Katelyn's journey underscores that success is not solely defined by medals or accolades but by one's ability to maintain a healthy relationship with oneself. She has shown that pursuing excellence while prioritizing self-care is possible, fostering an environment where individuals can thrive as competitors and as people.

Moreover, Katelyn's advocacy work goes beyond mere awareness; it ignites a call to action for change within sports organizations, educational institutions, and society. By emphasizing the necessity of mental health resources and support systems, she has inspired a movement to create a culture that values authenticity and compassion. Katelyn envisions a future where athletes are equipped with the tools they need to navigate their mental health and where they can feel empowered to embrace their identities without fear of judgment or reprisal.

The impact of Katelyn's story is profound. It encourages athletes and non-athletes to embrace their uniqueness and reject harmful beauty standards. Her commitment to body positivity resonates with many, challenging individuals to celebrate their bodies for what they can achieve rather than how they appear. By sharing her narrative of self-acceptance, Katelyn has inspired others to embark on their journeys toward confidence and empowerment.

Katelyn's legacy is not confined to her athletic achievements; it is also shaped by her role as a changemaker and advocate. She continues to engage in public speaking, writing, and community outreach, utilizing her platform to spread awareness about the issues that matter most to her. Through her efforts, Katelyn has fostered a sense of community among athletes and advocates, encouraging collaboration and support in the fight against mental health and body image stigma.

Katelyn's vision for the future is filled with hope and determination. She recognizes that the work is far from over and remains committed to making a lasting impact. By engaging with the next generation of athletes, Katelyn aims to instill the values of resilience, self-acceptance, and mental well-being in those who follow in her footsteps. Her story is a guiding light, reminding us of the importance of staying true to ourselves and supporting one another in our journeys.

Katelyn Ohashi's narrative is a testament to the power of vulnerability and authenticity. By sharing her story, she has transformed her life and ignited a movement that encourages others to embrace their true selves. Her commitment to advocating for mental health and body positivity challenges the status quo, pushing us to reconsider how we view success and worthiness. Katelyn's legacy empowers individuals to break free from societal constraints and pursue their passions with courage and integrity.

Reflecting on Katelyn's incredible journey, we must recognize that her impact extends beyond her athletic accomplishments. She is a beacon of hope, reminding us that it is possible to forge our paths and make a difference in the world. Her unwavering spirit and dedication to advocacy serve as a powerful call to action for all of us to contribute to a more inclusive and compassionate society. Katelyn Ohashi's story is not just her own; it is a shared narrative that encourages us to embrace our identities and champion the values of empathy, acceptance, and resilience.

Made in the USA
Las Vegas, NV
29 March 2025